PENGUIN BOOKS

## YOU ALL SPOKEN HERE

Roy Wilder, Jr., is a native of North Carolina, a self-described backsliding Methodist and yellow-dog Democrat. He has worked as a war correspondent, as a newspaper reporter for the *New York Herald Tribune*, as a political consultant, and as a public relations man. He lives in Gourd Hollow, just a howdy and a half from Spring Hope, North Carolina 27882.

# You All Spoken Here

## Roy Wilder, Jr.

*Foreword by*
*Willard R. Espy*

•

*Illustrations by*
*Glen Rounds*

•

PENGUIN BOOKS

PENGUIN BOOKS

Viking Penguin Inc., 40 West 23rd Street,
New York, New York 10010, U.S.A.
Penguin Books Ltd, Harmondsworth,
Middlesex, England
Penguin Books Australia Ltd, Ringwood,
Victoria, Australia
Penguin Books Canada Limited, 2801 John Street,
Markham, Ontario, Canada L3R 1B4
Penguin Books (N.Z.) Ltd, 182–190 Wairau Road,
Auckland 10, New Zealand

First published in the United States of America
by Viking Penguin Inc. 1984
Published in Penguin Books 1985

LIBRARY OF CONGRESS CATALOGING IN PUBLICATION DATA
Wilder, Roy.
You all spoken here.
Reprint. Originally published: New York, N.Y., U.S.A.: Viking, 1984.
1. English language—Provincialisms—Southern States—Dictionaries.
2. English language—Terms and phrases—Dictionaries.
I. Title. [PE2926.W5    1985]    427′.975    85-9454
ISBN 0 14 00.8404 5

Portions of the text of this book originally appeared in booklet form as follows: *You All Spoken Here, First Verse; You All Spoken Here, Second Verse;* and *You All Spoken Here, Third Verse,* copyright© Roy Wilder, Jr., 1975, 1976, 1977.

Printed in the United States of America by
R. R. Donnelley & Sons Company, Harrisonburg, Virginia
Set in ITC Cheltenham Light

For two who'd do to ride the river with:

*Glen Rounds*

*and*

*Willard R. Espy*

# Foreword

The time is the middle of the nineteenth century. The place is Virginia City, Nevada, site of the legendary Comstock silver lode. The characters are a gentle young minister, fresh from an Eastern theological seminary, and a hard-fisted, hard-drinking silver miner, Scotty. The writer is Mark Twain:

"Are you the duck that runs the gospel-mill next door?"

"Am I the—pardon me, I believe I do not understand?"

With another sigh and a half-sob, Scotty rejoined: "Why you see we are in a bit of trouble, and the boys thought maybe you would give us a lift, if we'd tackle you—that is, if I've got the rights of it, and you are the head clerk of the doxology-works next door."

"I am the shepherd in charge of the flock whose fold is next door."

"The which?"

"The spiritual adviser of the little company of believers whose sanctuary adjoins these premises."

Scotty scratched his head, reflected a moment, and then said: "You ruther hold over me, pard. I reckon I can't call that hand. Ante and pass the buck."

"How? I beg pardon. What did I understand you to say?"

"Well, you've ruther got the bulge on me. Or maybe we've both got the bulge, somehow. You don't smoke me, and I don't smoke you. You see, one of the boys has passed in his checks, and we want to give him a good send-off, and so the thing I'm on now is to roust out somebody to jerk a little chin-music for us and waltz him through handsome."

"My friend, I seem to grow more bewildered. Your observations are wholly incomprehensible to me."

It turns out that Scotty wants the minister to conduct a funeral service for a friend who had died a violent death, and who was ". . . the bulliest man in the mountains, pard! He could run faster, jump higher, hit harder, and hold more tanglefoot whisky without spilling it than any man in seventeen counties."

As Mark Twain demonstrates, regional language can be all but incomprehensible to an outsider. Once mined, though, it often turns out to be a veritable Comstock lode of metaphor and broad humor. Speech is silver, after all.

I was only eight years old when I first read the above passage (from *Roughing It*), and I have been prospecting for regionalisms ever since.

I chortle over the dialect of Maryland—"Balamer" for Baltimore, "doll" for dial, "clays" for clothes, "liggle" for legal.

And of Texas, where "ails" means else, "beggar," bigger, and "fair," fear.

And of Charleston, where "abode" is a wooden plank, and "ain't" is the sister of one of your parents.

And of New England, where they say "What in tunket got you so riled up?" and "Shouldn't wonder but what I will."

But I had never come across Tar Heel speech until a friend sent me a pamphlet by Roy Wilder, Jr., called *You All Spoken Here*. It turned out to be a rich lode indeed.

# Foreword

Can you resist such pungencies as "He's three pickles shy of a barrel" for someone a little less than bright? "Don't get cross-legged" for don't lose your temper? "A rubber-nosed woodpecker in a petrified forest" for an incompetent person? I can't.

So when I heard that Mr. Wilder was expanding his pamphlet into a book, I was quick to ask for a look at the manuscript. As you are about to see for yourself, it is a joy.

Roy Wilder knows what he is writing about. He is a native of North Carolina—a backsliding Methodist and yellow-dog Democrat. Exile in New York as a newspaperman and in the European theater of World War II as a press officer only proved to him that by comparison with the pure silver of North Carolina, the rest of the world speaks a clanking alloy. So he went home and wrote this book, to share his fortune with the Philistines.

Mark Twain would have loved *You All Spoken Here*. So will you.

*Willard R. Espy*

# Contents

# Contents

## But First, a Word from the Author

Leveling off.

That's what our nation's language has been doing lately.

As professors and earned-degree word-watchers put it, the language of the contiguous United States is "diminishing in diversity."

Time and television are apparently the major culprits in eroding our linguistic heritage. They make the national tongue as homogenized and bland as blue john and grits.*

But be not dismayed. The prospect is not altogether dismal. We have the happy privilege of reporting that colorless communication is not yet a complete national blight. Nosiree Bob.

Right here and now we are driving up a stob to inform the world that no matter how the outer precincts of the nation may fare with diluted diction, we in the South will have no part of it. Raised up right, we are sticking with our heritage. And be-

---

*Blue john is skimmed milk; grits are (is) an almost tasteless cereal, made palatable by applications of butter or assorted gravies.

cause of our bringing up, Southern speech today is alive and doing well, thanky—colorful, concise, irreverent, extravagant, bright-eyed, and bushy-tailed.

With two strong traditions—talking, and standing up and being counted—and with two stout articles to sustain us— corn bread and corn whiskey—we in the South aren't about to surrender. Not again. We refuse to knuckle under to stylebook-bound semanticists. We refuse to liquidate our native tongue, diverse and tatterdemalion though it may be. We respect and appreciate our honorable linguistic roots. We won't scorn them. We are just natured that way.

Professors, folklorists, and linguists all tell us that our speech—Southern speech—is the speech of olden days. They tell us that in our mountain coves, in our baronial textile-mill towns, at crossroads cotton gins, in backwater precincts, and in meetings of the United Daughters of the Confederacy, our way of speaking is the way it was with Chaucer and with Eliza-beth the Virgin Queen. Archaic English.

They tell us that Southern speech is the speech of the south of England, of Devon and Cornwall, of Wiltshire and Hamp-shire. The speech of Oxford, Cambridge, Stratford-on-Avon. Old World words, old phrases, old pronunciations that are Middle English or Mercian. They tell us, too, that Southern speech is the speech of the Border Country, of the Highland Scots and the so-called Scotch-Irish of Ulster. And lately the professors have come to recognize that Southern speech also contains an infusion of words and phrases introduced by slave culture. Many of these words have Arabic roots.

For generations we have preserved ancient accents, re-gional dialects, and colloquialisms. Many of the words and phrases in common and maybe not-so-common use are cen-turies old. We use words prefixed by the Middle English "a," and words with strong "ars." And bobtailed words without the "ars" and without the "gees" that weren't there in the first place. We use what H. L. Mencken called "gypsy phrases" with the "loose and brilliant syntax" of the seventeenth century.

# But First, a Word from the Author

We keep adding to our plunder room of usable materials, for ours is a viable language. We give ear to new phrases constructed in new times in new situations. If apprentice terms strike our fancy and survive the tests of time and usage, or wear and tear, we absorb them.

Here in the South, where there is more folk speech than anywhere else, we have no problem in accumulating new verbal goods. We aren't inhibited in our talk. We turn the spigot and let it burble. Some of our expressions are almost as old as our hills, but with proper application they sound just minted. In our flow of talk there often are phrases full of humor, of poetry, of beauty. There is speech soft and fluid. There is speech irreverent and impertinent, brash with bogus insults and mock abuse. Country humor is found in much of our talk, often earthy and seldom subtle, for pallid and insipid observations aren't inherent in our make of expression.

Here in this collation, this contribution to culture, we are, as we said earlier, driving up a stob. To make a statement.

We aren't about to back off from our linguistic heritage. Further, it is appropriate that at this the start of the four hundredth anniversary of the coming of the English to America—to North Carolina—we invite folks from the outer precincts and other foreign parts to lend an ear to what four centuries of Southern talk have wrought.

The collecting of these entries, these samples of words and phrases in Southern talk, was, at first, easy for us. It began with a book—the post office says that twenty-four pages constitute a book, and this was of twenty-four pages—a book produced to sell to tourists to prove they had been somewhere. The text came from words and phrases used and heard in our raisin' up in a small and rural town in North Carolina. . . .

The words and phrases came from talk at The Honey Hole, a service (gasoline) station the May boys operated. It was across the street from the post office where my father had been postmaster. Most every male in the trading area, preachers and dogs included, got by The Honey Hole most every day or so. For a gallon or so of gas, a co-cola, and to check on what was doin' hereabouts. Much of the conversation pertained to tobacco crops and cotton futures, to fishin', fightin', an' makin' out. . . .

More talk of native turn came in canvassing the countryside in a Model-T sedan, picking up clothes for dry cleaning in Zeke Bunn's pressing club, situated in a business district by name of Graball. . . .

Years in newspapering and political campaigning in these parts and abroad brought more memorable words and phrases into the conversational pot. . . .

And reading. It's surprising what you can learn if you read newspapers, books, magazines. And if you discriminate in television fare. We find linguistic treasures in diverse places: in free-ranging columns and editorials in regional newspapers by writers such as William Murchison, Jack Aulis, John Terry, Jack Leland, Roy Thompson, Guy Friddell, Jerry Bledsoe, Lindsey Nelson, Joe Creason, John Parris, Jim Shumaker, Dennis Rogers, Lawrence Maddry, Kays Gary, Bill Horner, Don Whitehead, Dot Jackson . . . in regional magazines such as *The State* (Raleigh, N.C.) and *Emory Magazine* (Atlanta, Ga.) . . . in the WPA guides to states, the various *Foxfire* publications, the *American Folkways* series, the *States and the Nation* series, the *Rivers of America* series . . . in forgotten and obscure books come to light in flea markets, yard sales, used book stores . . . in regional books . . . vanity books . . . *Verbatim* . . . jobs of word work by Stuart Berg Flexner, H. L. Mencken, Ernie Deane, M. M. Mathews, Rogers Whitener, John S. Farmer, William and Mary Morris . . . publications of the American Dialect Society . . . *Western Words* by Ramon F. Adams . . . J. R. Bartlett's *Dictionary of Americanisms* . . . Norman E. Eliason's *Tarheel Talk* . . . the *Frank C. Brown Collection of North Carolina Folklore* . . . *Down in the Holler* by Vance Randolph and George P. Wilson . . . and *Slang and Its Analogues*. . . .

Surprising, too, is what you can learn from just plain keeping an ear turned and tuned for comment. Call it eavesdropping or researching, it is rewarding. Like idling in a shopping mall and hearing, "He's jus' loudin' off." And in an elevator in Mobile, "Her nose was drippin' like a' ash hopper." In the Sykes Seed Store in my hometown, when the Symposium of Stove-huggers gathers of a cold morning, you can hear such as "Rest yore coat," inviting a newcomer to pull up a chair and join the loafers, and, "North Carolinians used to believe in hell, calomel, and the Democratic party, they shore did."

And letters . . . In producing and in peddling a trilogy of books on corn-pone talk, we got hundreds of letters from around the nation and abroad. Some complained; most offered contributions: something Gran'pa used to say in Alabama . . . terminology in discussing coon dogs, rabbit dogs, bird dogs . . . some sayings from North Georgia . . . textile mill talk . . . comment on the derivation of particular words and phrases . . . footnote material. . . . Also, "You didn't say it right," and, "You've substituted filth for humor."

Whatever our faults of admission and omission, of translation and definition, we have presented here a cornucopia of collector's items that can be rewarding to natives as well as newcomers from the outside world. It is a guide to carryin' on and making' out in Southern states.

Who knows but what you may laugh rather than take umbrage when confronted of a sudden by our ribald humor, or what one of us, Irvin S. Cobb, called "scaly-barked wisdom."

And perhaps you may comprehend at first blush a peculiarly Southern culinary idiom: How come, when you order ham and eggs in Southern eateries, the platter most always comes with a dollop of unrequested grits?

Have fun, you all . . . heah?

*Roy Wilder, Jr.*

*Gourd Hollow*
*Spring Hope, North Carolina*

# You All
# Spoken
# Here

# Character and Personality Defined Flat Out

*There was this dude from Up North who'd been places an' et in ho-tels. He had swung a wide loop and heard the hoot owls hoot in a lot of places. He let you know he'd been around. And now he was visiting his wife's folks in a farming community in the South. His wife was well fixed: sole heir to some two-horse farms with good bottom land, rental property in town, and the ultimate in status symbols—two cars and a boat.*

*The visitor was nosy about the man who had accumulated these worldly goods, and he inquired of one who had known him well.*

*He asked, flat out, if his wife's father was a crook.*

*The man who had left his daughter well fixed was country smart, the visitor was told. He had a distant turn and wasn't mightily beliked, but he was sharp as a briar. He had run a time store business, furnishing farm supplies, fertilizer, mules, and provisions for farm owners and tenants. He wasn't a crook, nosiree Bob, but he often operated on the rim edge of*

1

*the law. Now and then it looked like he measured t'other fel-
ler's corn to his own bushel.*

*"He was a close chewer an' a tight spitter," said the man
who had known him well. "He took in a lot of mules."*

Too poor to paint, too proud to whitewash: Southern aristocracy.

Pore mouthin': Someone pleading poverty when he's got a
sight of money—he's got enough money to burn a wet
mule.

Purse proud: Stingy; grasping; graspious; brags of how much
money he's got laid back.

Tight: Stingy; he's so tight, when he grins his pecker skins
back; she makes pancakes so thin they've got just one side
to them; he's so tight, when he blinks his eyes his toes curl.

Tight as a tick: Frugal; close with a dollar. When President
Carter personally ordered American officials in London
to transfer to less expensive hotels, Press Secretary Jody
Powell said of him, "He's tight as a tick." When pressed to
explain the term, Powell said, "It means he's cheap."

A close chewer and a tight spitter: Same as above.

He breathes through his nose to keep from wearing out his
false teeth: He's so stingy he squeaks when he walks; he's
too stingy to give you the time of day; he'd skin a flea for the
hide and tallow.

Chinchy: Said of a skinflint; he's so chinchy, he can call his
every dollar by its first name.

Close: Parsimonious; miserly; a near man with a dollar.

Snudge: Miser.

Ready with his hat and slow with his money: Courteous and close-fisted.

Wants the earth an' the moon with two strands of bobwire aroun' it—an' it whitewashed: Greedy.

Stiff in the heels: Has money; is well fixed.

Slick: Sharp; so slippery he'd hold his own in a pond full of eels; he's slicker than a greased eel.

He ain't a man to tie to in a calm much less a storm, he'll never do to tie to: Untrustworthy; unreliable.

He lies like a rug: He's a flat-out liar; he lies so bad he hires somebody to call his dogs.

His mouth ain't no prayerbook: Same as above.

His uncle stole my grandpap's horse: You wouldn't trust him behind a broomstraw; he'd steal as you looked at him.

Narrow between the eyes: Not to be trusted.

A good face and a bad heart: Deceitful.

He took in a lot of mules: He wasn't a crook but was quick to foreclose on farmers.

He's low-down as a snake in a wagon track: He could wear a top hat and walk under a snake's belly.

Grand rascal: A cheat; a scoundrel.

He'll measure t'other feller's grain to his bushel: He's a cheat; he'll give himself the advantage.

He's so crooked he couldn't sleep in a roundhouse: He's as crooked as a barrel full of fish hooks; he's as crooked as a live oak limb.

He and the devil drink through the same quill: He's mean and sorry as the devil.

Spendthrifty: Extravagant, as someone with too many credit cards.

Bone carrier, trash toter: A gossip, like a dog carrying a bone.

Sand toter: An informer.

Notional: One who acts when he takes a notion to and not before.

His head is full of stump water: He doesn't have as much sense as you could slap in a gnat's ass with a butter paddle; an idea would bust his head wide open.

He's as bright as a burned-out light bulb: Dumber than a bushel and a peck and a gourd's neck.

If brains were dynamite he wouldn't have enough to blow his nose: He doesn't have sense enough to grease a gimlet; if a bird had his brains he'd fly back'ards.

He was behind the door when brains were passed out: If his brain was put on a fork it would look like BB shot rolling down a four-lane highway.

He won't get bow-legged totin' his brains: He ain't got a case of the smarts; he don't know shit from Shinola.

No more sense than last year's bird nest: Don't know split beans from coffee.

He couldn't teach a settin' hen to cluck: He has a bad case of the simples.

He couldn't organize a piss-off in a brewery: He couldn't grow pole beans in a pile of horse shit.

He couldn't find his ass with both hands in broad daylight: He couldn't pour piss from a boot with directions printed on the heel.

His egg got shook: He's uncoordinated.

He's three pickles shy of a barrel, he's three brick shy of a load: He's a drop button; he's kind of cracky.

His traces ain't hooked up right: He's not playing with a full deck; he ain't got all his marbles; his brain is wrapped loose; his roof ain't nailed on tight.

He's got just one oar in the water: He's crippled where a walking stick won't help him; he's half a bubble out of plumb.

He could mess up a rainstorm, he could mess up a one-car funeral: He couldn't hit a bull in the ass with a bass fiddle; he couldn't hit the ground if he fell; clumsy; inept.

Gower: Clumsy.

A terrible hand: Same as above; "he's a terrible hand at reloading shotgun shells—all thumbs."

Cymlin head: Dolt; dumber than a barrel of hair. Cymlin is an old word for squash.

Empty stack: Not much upstairs.

Half-baked: Immature; product of fuzzy thinking.

Half-cocked: Ill prepared; doesn't know "B" from bull's foot.

Light-minded: Light-headed; flighty.

Swarved up: Confused.

Mizzled: Muddled.

Startenated fool: Someone as foolish now as when dropped from his mammy's womb.

Scoggin: A butt for ridicule; a buffoon.

Crazy as a bedbug: Turn a light on a bedbug in a bed and he runs ever' which-a-way, like crazy.

> The June bug has golden wings,
> The lightning bug the flame;
> The bed bug has no wings at all,
> But he gets there just the same.
> —An old refrain

Slap-assed crazy: What tourists make Billy Carter.

He can see through hog wire: He isn't the smartest gent to come up the road, but he gets the message.

He's got sense enough to keep out of the fire: Same as above.

He don't wear no blinders: He's smart, sees everything.

Smart as a tree full of owls: Has more information than a mail-order catalog.

Sharp as a briar: Smart as a whip; has a brain as quick as a steel trap.

He gets down to where the water hits the wheel: He gets to the root of the matter, the seat of the problem, where the action is.

He's all sorts of a feller: He's an expert. Experts know more of less.

Country smart: With superior native intelligence. Such as pitcher Catfish Hunter, who broke the price barrier with better than three million dollars to throw hardball, and the Dukes of Durham, who made it big in tobacco, textiles, and electric power.

Country boy: Someone who gains the upper hand by playing dumb. President Lyndon Johnson once advised, "When somebody tells you he's a country boy, keep your hand on your pocketbook."

Few weevils in his wheat: Said of a decent, exemplary citizen.

Mighty small chance of water in his whiskey: Same as above.

Not a drop of streaked blood in his veins, the clean fur: Upright; of unblemished character.

He always goes by his own name: He's an honorable person; he wouldn't cheat you of nary a grain of corn.

He plows a straight furrow and goes to the end of the row: He's honest, dependable; he'll accomplish his assignment.

Bound and determined: Committed, come hell and high water.

He can pack a saw log to hell and back before breakfast: He can handle tough assignments.

He stacked muskets at Appomattox: An honorable badge to those who plowed to the end of the row. Ben Ames Williams wrote, "To have been paroled at Appomattox was not enough, since many of those were weaponless stragglers. But to have 'stacked muskets at Appomattox' meant that men had not only endured, but had carried their weapons and kept themselves in fighting trim."

He'll do to ride the river with: You can trust him, can depend on him, despite adversity. This is a phrase favored by Lady Bird Johnson. It is, wrote Ramon F. Adams, "about the highest compliment that can be paid a cowman. It originated back in the old trail days when brave men had to swim herds across swollen, treacherous rivers. The act required level-headed courage, and as time passed, this phrase meant that the one spoken of was loyal, dependable, trustworthy, and had plenty of sand."

He's a man you'd go to the well with: Same as above. From frontier days, when the person toting water from the well appreciated the company of somebody riding shotgun;

somebody who would share the risks and stand with you under duress.

He'll make the trip: He will succeed; he is dependable. The expression comes from flat-boating: despite the hazards, he will make the float downstream and return safely. Back in the spring of 1828, some said that Southern-born Abraham Lincoln, then nineteen years old, would make the trip from Kentucky down the Mississippi to New Orleans, and he did.

He'd stand in the hedge and take up the gap: He's a staunch defender. Leon Jaworski, a Texan and the Watergate prosecutor who forced President Nixon to resign, was described thusly at his funeral.

He totes the key to the smokehouse: He's trustworthy, has privileged information.

He could borrow salt: Said of a visitor so prized he'd be welcome to share bed and board for at least three days.

Top sawyer: The top man, the most skillful, in a pit-sawing operation; to call one a top sawyer in any line of work is a compliment.

He keeps his corners up: He keeps his property and affairs in good order.

Two-button man: One of little consequence; one who has to loosen only two buttons of his fly to relieve himself or engage in what was known in World War II as "hasty field fornication."

Four-button man: A real stud.

Quar-turned an' droll-natured: Said of someone who hears a different drummer.

Has a master hand for notions: Has fanciful ideas, a head full of notions.

He had a lot of sour pudding stuck in his head: Same as above.

Common: Unassuming; without put-on or airs; ordinary. "When you come right down to it, our governor is jist as common as you and me."

Common: Trashy; not worth two hoots in hell; not worth the shot it would take to kill him; common as pig tracks or goat nuts. "That's a right common crowd over yonder. Sorry as all get out."

Won't amount to a hill of beans: Worthless; won't amount to a row of pins.

Sorry: Of poor quality; lazy; incompetent as a right sorry jack-leg carpenter, or a ditch-bank blacksmith, or a shade-tree mechanic.

Suggin: Of low mentality; of poor stock. "They's a fambly over toward Whistleberry that's all suggins. They've married each other so much they all got six toes an' six fingers."

He's an empty sack: He's triflin'; no 'count; ain't worth gully dirt.

He ain't worth shucks: He's sorry, good for nothing, not worth dried spit.

Triflin': Worthless; not fit to carry guts to a bear; ain't worth a milk bucket under a bull. If you're triflin' trash, you're common as dish water, sorry as owl bait.

He'll never set a river a-fire with a split match: He won't amount to much.

He's a good ol' dog but he don't like to hunt: He's affable and plum' lazy.

Workbrickle: Sort of lazy.

He'll never drown in sweat: He's too lazy to hit a lick at a snake; he's as slow as cream a-rising.

He's so lazy he stops plowin' to fart: He's so lazy he wouldn't get his breath if it didn't come natch'l.

He hasn't got the spirit to lift a louse off a hot griddle: Listless; he'd starve to death in a pie factory.

Lazy as a tarred hog: Tired and indifferent. Tar is often used as an antiseptic in bucolic surgery, such as castrations; experts in the procedure are known as "pig trimmers." (Cutting, or castration, is ill-advised when the sign of the Zodiac is in Scorpio, the sign ruling the reproductive organs.)

He's so slow the dead lice fall off him: He's so slow you have to set up stakes to see if he's moving.

Born tired and never got rested: Born lazy and had a bad setback; born in the middle of the week and looking both ways for Sunday; too lazy to say "sooey" if the hogs were eating him.

Lookin' for sundown an' payday: Piddlin'; doesn't exert himself while on the job.

He follows the shade around the house: He avoids physical labor.

He's drunk on chimney smoke: He won't work outdoors during inclement weather.

Seben sleeper: Someone who sleeps like the dead; someone abed when he should be up and doing. From the Seven Sleepers of Ephesus, who awoke after two centuries and testified to the doctrine of the resurrection and the body.

Antsy: Like a child fidgeting in church; fidgety as a grasshopper.

Feisty: Spirited; full of beans; running on three legs and pretending much. Comes from "fisting dog" ("fistan," to break wind), an aggressive and flatulent little mongrel, or a fice.

Strut fart, a: One highly conscious of his own importance.

Georgia major: A pretentious man. Ben Ames Williams reports
that after passage of the Confederacy's conscription law of
1864, Governor Joseph E. Brown of Georgia "took advantage of the exemption granted state militia officers" and is-
sued commissions to some 3,000 friends. Thus a lavish of
Georgia majors.     ˙

Governor Brown also fathered "Joe Brown's pikes."
Under the mistaken idea that the medieval pike would be
an effective nineteenth-century infantry weapon, he had
thousands of them produced by some one hundred sup-
pliers. None was used in combat. John Brown, no relation
to the Georgia governor but a contemporary and better
known for his trek from Osawatomie to Harper's Ferry, also
favored pikes.

Brigaty: Self-important; wants to show off; haughty; arrogant.

Biggity, biggedy: Same as above.

Uppity: Above his raising.

All vines and no taters: Only a facade, a false front.

All hat and no cattle: Texian for the above.

He's been places an' et in ho-tels: He's sophisticated.

He swung a wide loop and heard the hoot owls hoot in a lot of
places: He's a man what's been around. Some who swung a
wide loop were regarded as cattle thieves, rustling somebody else's cattle, and some who heard the hoot owls hoot
were known to drink to excess.

Dirt road sport: A country boy showing off in a Saturday afternoon town.

Struttin' like a rooster: High-stepping, especially if wearing a jim-swinger, or a claw hammer, or a graveyard duster—a split-tailed coat.

Tail up and stinger out: Full of piss and vinegar; aggressive; ready to go and fit for most anything; has git up an' go.

Spry as a basket of chips: Chipper; alert.

His tail is over the dashboard: He's in high spirits.

She ain't easy to break to halter: She's high-spirited.

He's got his ass on his shoulders: He's fractious.

She's a honey but the bees don't know it: She carries herself proud; she thinks a right smart of herself.

High-nosed: Same as above.

Mincy: Fastidious; finicky; picky; she's so persnickety she wouldn't be happy in a pie factory.

Prissy: Prim; finicky.

She turns the corners square: She thinks she's the only huckleberry on the bush.

Miratin': Expressing wonderment and surprise; admiring, as one who appreciates himself. "He who tooteth not his own horn, the same will not get tooted"—an old quotation.

Boring with a big auger: Trying to exceed one's capabilities; acting with a flourish.

Above my huckleberry: Above my bend; beyond my reach; past my ability.

He's trying to fart higher than his ass: He's hanging the basket higher than he can reach.

He's trying to ride a high horse when he couldn't ride a calf: Same as above.

He overwound his watch: He over did it.

He was raised on firebread an' soppin' gravy, an' she was raised on ham an' eggs: He married above hisself. Firebread is bread cooked on an open fire for lack of a stove or a Dutch oven.

He's weeding a wide row: He's running roughshod; he's cutting a wide swath.

Captain of the corn pile: At the corn shuckin' he traipsed on top of the pile, led the singing, made the most noise, worked the least.

Got a lot of gall: Impudent; brassy; bold as a burglar.

Nibby: Inquisitive; meddlesome.

Whippersnapper: A flashy and noisy young man.

Brassy: With excessive assurance; unpleasantly aggressive; brazen; cheeky; pushy.

Corinthian brass: Same as above. "Corinthian brass, that's what she is. Shameless. Absolutely shameless."

Tacky: Not couth; out of place; improper.

Chewed tobacco fast: Was angered but kept it under control.

Had a fartin' spell: Displayed bad temper; showed his ass.

Tore up the patch: Same as above.

Got all bent out of shape: Ditto.

He was spittin' worse'n a goose, he was spittin' like a goose a-shittin' by moonlight: So angry he frothed at the mouth.

Fitified: Temperamental; inclined to have tantrums and fits.

Spittin' cotton: Expectorating freely when angry or excited; also pertains to the next morning's nest-in-the-mouth dryness after drinking too much corn whiskey.

His snuff's too strong: He's so angry he can't spit straight.

Ambition: A grudge, as "I had an ambition against him."

Ambitious: Angry; enraged; aggressive.

Raised his gorge: Angered, embarrassed, or disgusted him so much it made his Adam's apple bobble and made him want to puke.

High-tempered: Has a short fuse.

All fire and tow: About to explode. "Tow" is a fiber of flax, hemp, and jute good for starting fires and used for patches in firing muzzle-loading rifles.

Savagerous: Ferocious.

Gone haywire: Gone all askew.

Ills: Annoys; irritates; angers, as "It ills me to hear jocks talk on the tee-vee when their dialogue consists mostly of 'you know.'"

Sand in his craw, sand in his gizzard: Fractious.

Mighty pestering: Annoying; bedeviling.

Beflustered: Flabbergasted.

Flustrated, flusterated: Greatly agitated; checked.

Put out: Vexed; exasperated.

Faultin' person, a: A constant nag; a complainer; someone who'd complain even if you hung him with a bran' new plow line.

Don't sit horses together: Unneighborly; don't have much to do with each other.

Hardness: Bad feelings between people; bad blood between families.

Severe: Fractious; wild; cross.

Strong-minded: Strong-willed.

He sets his mind: His mind's made up; he's determined, stubborn.

A fly-up-the-creek: One likely to change his mind.

To sull: To sulk, be sullen or pouty; to flat-out stop and not go; a horse that sulls wouldn't budge enough to break an egg under his collar. If a horse, mule, or steer sulls and flops down and won't budge, he will get a move on if you rook him. To rook a recalcitrant, you poke dry leaves under his tail, get a good hold on the reins, and set the leaves on fire.

Nellify: Balk and refuse to go forward.

Stubborn as a blue-nosed mule: More stubborn than anything. A blue-nosed mule isn't blue-nosed, but black-nosed like an ordinary mule. The coat of an ordinary mule is brown or gray or mottled black, but the coat of a blue-nosed mule is solid coal-black. Okay?

Offish, stand-offish: Reserved.

Turn: A talent, manner, or instinct for, as "Bob Scott an' Pat Taylor have a turn for doin' the right thing—almost ever' time near 'bout."

Have a distant turn: Have a haughty manner; be aloof; not much for neighboring.

Have a friendly turn: Opposite of above, as one could have "as friendly a turn as ever you'd see."

Turn a hand: Produce; work.

A good hand for: Adapted for; cut out for, as "I ain't no good hand for stayin' up all night at no likker still."

Clever: Said of one who can turn his hand to almost any project.

Clever: Obliging; generous; amiable; neighborly; clever hosts put strangers at ease.

Cute as a bug's ear: Cute as a bug in a rug.

Disencouraged: Discouraged; pessimistic; down in the mouth; out of heart.

Grum and chuff: Morose and forbidding; sulky; surly; coarse; blunt.

He looks like he eats green persimmons three times a day: Same as above.

A woman jessy: A coward.

Softish: Sissified.

Feather-legged: Craven; cowardly. Comes from cockfighting, or cocking: a cock with feathered legs is a poor performer in the pit.

Slack-twisted: Lacking in courage; said of someone who makes false excuses for failures; one who feigns excuses to escape military duty. Comes from spinning and weaving in cottage operations: cloth from insufficiently twisted thread does not wear well.

Step to: Obey; dance to the tune called by a rich widow.

Her tongue wags at both ends: Her mouth is runnin' up a storm.

Her tongue is tied in the middle and wagging at both ends: She must have been vaccinated with a Victrola needle.

She would talk the legs off a stove: Same as above.

Runnin' on: Doin' a piece of talkin'.

He's passin' gas faster'n he can cap it: Oilfield talk for a windbag.

16

He don't use up his kindlin' to get a fire started: Said of a man of few words.

Broadspoken: Outspoken; uses coarse language.

All fired up: Excited.

Proud: Pleased; also means being in heat.

Journey proud: Excited or bragging about a trip made or anticipated.

Kindly: Graciously.

She'll take in the slack: She has sufficient attributes to make up for the deficiencies of her husband—as do some preachers' wives.

In a clean spot: On good behavior.

He's enough to make a dog laugh: He's a cut-up; a card; a real caution; one who cuts the fool.

Mess, a: A person regarded as more witty, more lively, more entertaining than others, as in "That Lindsey Nelson, now . . . ain't he ever more a pure livin' mess?"

Mightily beliked: Popular.

Juneing around: Flitting leisurely, as a June bug with a length of tobacco twine connecting a leg to a child at the other end. June bugs with gardenhouse odor are called tumble turds.

Givey: Unsteady, as a just-dropped calf or a bar patron.

Did him dirt: Treated him shabbily.

Carries her on a pillow: Said of one who is ostentatiously considerate of a lady love.

Roguish: Thieving; mischievous.

They wash hands together: They are friends.

They wipe hands together: They are foes.

They piss through the same quill: They are like two peas in a pod—not a dime's difference between them; congenial; ass-hole buddies.

Couthy, couthie: Agreeable; friendly.

If you th'owed him in the river he'd float upstream: He's contrary.

If she gets to heaven she'll ask to see the upstairs: There's no pleasing that woman.

He wouldn't go to a funeral unless he could be the corpse: He's vain.

# The Word for Today and Other Sage Advices

*Ninety-five percent of all putts you leave short don't go in.*
                    —*Hubert Green, a professional*
                        *golfer from Birmingham,*
                        *Alabama*

*Don't talk back. Keep the woodbox filled. And don't stake the*
*cow where she can get to wild onions.*
                    —*Malcolm Buie Seawell, Jurist*
                        *and Attorney General of North*
                        *Carolina, on how to make*
                        *points with your mother*

Don't start chopping till you've treed the coon: Don't jump to conclusions; don't anticipate the command; be sure you've got the votes.

Never hallo till you are out of the woods: Same as above.

Never insult an alligator till you've crossed the stream: Ditto.

Never bet on taters a-fore grabblin' time: Don't count chickens before they hatch.

Don't ever count the crop till it's in the barn: Same as above. Mister Sam Rayburn, former Speaker of the House and veteran of life in East Tennessee and East Texas, often used the phrase.

Church ain't out till they quit singing: It ain't over till it's over, as Yogi Berra said.

Don't try to kill the snake unless you've got the hoe in your hands.

You can't measure a snake until it's stretched out dead.

Early don't last long.

Good likker needs no water.

The hair of the dog is good for the bite.

Dress up a dog and his tail will stick out.

The higher a monkey climbs the more he shows his ass.

Even in a dog fight a person has his druthers.

God gave nuts to them that's got no teeth.

You have to draw to ketch. Catch a winning hand in poker, that is.

Shoot or give up your gun: Work or hold the candle; talk or wave a bush; paint or get off the ladder, piss or get off the pot. President Abraham Lincoln put it this way when explaining the assignment of two of his generals, Butler and Sigel, to subordinate roles in an upcoming Civil War campaign: "Those not skinning can hold a leg."

The big coon walks late: The smart one reaps the reward. "Ain't no need to mess aroun' early of a night," said Orville Woodhouse, coon hunter. "That's when possums an' little coons get in the way."

The still sow gets the slops: Same as above.

Every crow thinks hers is blackest.

Kill another skunk: Create a diversion.

White mules never die: They become Baptist preachers.

Tote your own skillet.

Love many and trust few, and always paddle your own canoe.

Let every man skin his own skunk: Mind your own business.

Kill your own snake: Same as above.

Chew your own tobacco: Hoe your own row.

There's a whole new day tomorrow that ain't been touched yet.

Everybody has to look out of his own keyhole.

Don't get in a pissin' contest with a skunk.

You're whistling up a gum stump: You're wasting time and effort. Gum stumps are usually hollow.

This is no time to swap knives: Don't trade horses in midstream.

A short horse is soon curried.

It doesn't take long to examine a hot horseshoe.

It doesn't take long to work five minutes.

You can't churn butter from spilled milk: So don't cry over it.

If a toady frog had wings he wouldn't bump his ass: So make do with what you have.

Put it down where the goats can get it: Tell it out in front.

Let the milk down: Tell it all; don't hold back; wring it out.

Put it on the front porch: Let everybody know.

Them that don't pluck don't git feathers.

If you're bound to hang, you won't drown.

Keep your hook baited.

The dinner bell is always in tune.

Idleness wears out the frog's ass.

Sittin' is cheaper'n standin'.

Don't strain your egg bag: Don't try to kid me.

Every tub must stand on its own bottom.

Don't wait for your granny's sidesaddle: Sidesaddles are scarce as hen's teeth. A claim for North Carolina origin can be made for "scarce as hen's teeth." John Thomas Gatling, of Halifax County, North Carolina, used the term in a letter in 1858, five years earlier than the citation in the *Dictionary of Americanisms*.

Love God, hate the devil, and stay out of deadenin's in thunderstorms: A deadening is an area where trees are killed by girdling—by removing large areas of bark. Rotting limbs falling from deadened trees menace one's health and serenity. August is the best time to deaden trees, for sap has stopped seething and trees are dormant.

Remember to trust the Lord, write your mother, and vote the Democratic ticket.

To get clear water you've got to go to the head of the branch: Don't waste time with underlings; go to the top.

The water won't clear till you get the hogs out of the creek: Put your affairs in order; arrange your priorities.

Old rats like cheese, too.

Live one day at a time and scratch where it itches.

There are more ways to kill a cat than choke it to death with hot butter.

You can catch more flies with honey than with vinegar.

Whip a horse with oats.

A good way to catch a calf is to fling a nubbin to the cow: To court a daughter, be kind to her mother. A nubbin is an immature ear of corn, of little value.

Bait the cow to catch the calf: Same as above.

It'll never be noticed on a galloping horse: It's trivial; it is of no great importance.

When a pig's belly busts his body craves rest.

Creaking doors hang the longest: Frail folk often outlast the robust.

Soap your screws: Back up; cool off; readjust; start anew. Nails and screws that are smeared with lubricant are often more easily worked into hardwood.

Lick your flint and try again: Start over. In days of "long rifles," when the flint failed to strike fire and set off the powder charge, the way to insure a fat spark was to dampen the flint with the tongue and pull the trigger again.

It's a poor dog that can't wag its own tail.

It's a poor hen that can't scratch for one chick.

Kick off the harness, kick the traces: Throw off restraints.

Empty barrels make the loudest noise: He talks just to hear his head roar.

The longest pole knocks down the persimmons.

Don't hit a hornet's nest with a short stick.

Peel and whittle with a big blade.

Put the sawmill where the timber is.

There's a heap of whiskey spilt 'twixt the counter and the mouth.

Never thump a free watermelon: Don't look a gift horse in the mouth.

Fierce words need mending.

Them as is friends don't need no thanky.

What is to be will be, and what ain't ought to of been.

Sleep with a dog and you'll have fleas: The fleas come with the dog, every dog has a few fleas to scratch.

You needn't kick before you're spurred: You're ahead of the hounds.

A bossy woman and a crowing hen always come to a bad end.

A closed mouth gathers no foot: Put your mind in gear before talking.

Don't stir the turd: The more you stir, the more it stinks.

If it ain't chickens, it's feathers: That's life.

One day drinking wine, next day picking grapes: Same as above.

Treat mistakes like copperheads in bedclothes.

Never follow an empty wagon: Nothing falls off.

You can't catch a weasel asleep.

There's no use to have a dog and bark for one's self.

If you've got a rooster, he's going to crow.

If it ain't broke, don't fix it: Don't mess with a clock that runs on time.

Buzzards and chickens come home to roost: Your bad deeds will haunt you.

Hit's jes the way hit is: There's nothing you can do about it; it's a problem that defies solution.

Everything that goes around in the dark ain't Santa Claus.

You don't have to hang from a tree to be a nut.

A new broom sweeps clean, but the old one knows where the dirt is.

A man will overrun a heap more than he will overtake. Be quick but never hurry, was the way Coach John Wooden, of UCLA, put it.

With plenty of patience and plenty of vaseline, you can frig a cat.

Two heads are better than one, even if one is a sheep's head.

Don't dip your pen in the office ink: Steer clear of the hired help.

Watermelons don't grow on gourd vines.

Don't buy your ticket until the train is ready to pull out.

Stick with Terry and you'll fart through silk: Terry Sanford's cheerful admonition to spirit up the troops—in the 517th

Parachute Combat Team in World War II and in his political campaigns.

The look of the puddin' is not always the taste.

No dog ever enjoyed a hunt unless he could do some barking.

A chicken will fly around after its head is chopped off: Although the issue is settled, some folks will keep mouthin' about it.

When you go to a mule's funeral, weep at the front end.

Watch your mouth: Watch your language, especially if your vocabulary includes all the words and phrases in this contribution to culture.

# Domestic and Other Blisses Too Numerous to Mention

*If she ain't good enough fer her own folks, how do I know if she's good enough fer us?*

> —*A Tennessee mountaineer to his son who proposed to marry a certified virgin*

Reticule: A small bag, originally of net-work, favored by ladies who wear hats and gloves and tote parasols. A properly fitted reticule contains cologne, paregoric, liquid asafetida, and a silver spoon. Ms. Frances B. Denton of Austin, Texas, personal secretary to Colonel E. M. House when he was President Woodrow Wilson's confidant, protected his papers when they traveled with a small revolver that she toted in her reticule.

Poke: A sack or bag.

Go poke: A traveling bag.

Sanky poke: Thanky poke; a bag for the collecting of gifts.

Gritchel: A valise. The word is a contraction of grip and satchel.

Suggin, sujjit: A pouch; valise; carryall.

Redd up: Tidy up; straighten up.

Do: Wash, as in "Do the dishes, you hear?"

Do: Suffice; take care of; provide for, as in "A mess of collards will do us all."

Spread: Arrange; make, as in "Spread the bed."

Fix: Arrange; set, as in "Fix the dinner table."

Heading: A pillow.

She has everything up to now: She has everything in good order.

House moss, slut's wool, dust bunnies, turkey's nest, woolies: Piles of dust and lint.

Lick and a promise: The once-over-lightly housekeeping of bachelors and daytime-TV-watching maids.

Turn out a room: Rearrange the whole thing; move every stick of furniture.

Snake the kivvers: Before retiring, give the bedclothes a smart flirt to dislodge snakes that might've sneaked in.

Cat holes: Small openings in doors for ingress and egress of cats.

Spit holes: Apertures in cabin floors for disposal of snuff and chewing-tobacco cuds and juices.

Lay a fire: Put kindlin' and firewood in a stove or fireplace preparatory to igniting it with a striking match.

Striking match: Kitchen match, with wooden shaft. One that you can hold in the fingers of one hand and strike by flicking your thumbnail across the head is hard to come by nowadays. It's a farmer match in northern Illinois, a barn burner in western Pennsylvania.

Breakfast wood: Quick-burning firewood, such as dry pine.

Dinner wood: Long burning hardwoods, such as oak and hickory.

Roust up: Revive, as in getting a fire going from banked coals.

Chunk the fire: Add chunks of firewood.

Mend the fire, fix the fire: Tend the fire.

Board light: A lightwood knot used as a lighting device.

Clay the hearth: Paint the hearth with whitewash.

Cat and clayed: Refers to a chimney or a frame structure with an exterior covering of mud and sticks, or straw and clay, worked together. Jefferson Davis built a cat-and-clayed house in Mississippi.

Wattle and daub chimney: Same as above.

Tabby, tabby work, tapia: A concrete formed of a mixture of lime, shells, gravel, or stone, popular during Colonial days in the coastlands of the Carolinas and Georgia. "Tabby" is an Arabic word that passed into African language, thence into these parts via blacks.

Window lights: Window panes.

Pizer posts: Columns on piazzas, verandas, porches, galleries.

Piazza room, preacher's room: A small room at the end of and opening on the front porch.

Gallery: A porch, particularly an upstairs one, all the way around a house.

Story and a jump: A dwelling with an attic type, low-ceilinged room on the upper floor.

Knock-head room: One with a low ceiling.

Dog-trot house: A house of two one-room cabins joined by a roof, creating a dog trot, dog run, or breezeway between the two sections.

Saddlebag house, Texas house: Same as above.

Shotgun house: A low-cost, single-story, timbered residence, two and three rooms deep. It has no hallway, and doorways are in the middle of each room. They are shackly, as if constructed by throwing up old boards and nailing them together with charges of ten-penny nails blasted from a 12-gauge double-barreled shotgun—thus the name—and throwing on shingles during a high wind.

Shotgun houses were popular for textile plant housing and lumber camps, and for cheap housing in cities such as Memphis and New Orleans. Some shotgun houses today in New Orleans are showplaces, with Greek Revival decorations, galleries, stained-glass windows, and jigsaw work.

Some say the shotgun tag was applied because one could fire a shotgun charge through the front door and it would go out the back without hitting anything or anybody. Whoever believes the theory knows little about ever-widening shot patterns.

Camelback houses: A New Orleans variety of back-to-back rows of shotgun houses, built one story in front, two stories in back—thus the camel hump.

The houses used to have an ingenious feature: double-decker privies to serve four families. Ground-floor patrons trotted across the back yard, while upstairs people risked plank walkways suspended in midair. Gardyloo— look out for the slops!

Whistle walk: The walkway on plan'ation establishments between the big house and the detached kitchen. Servants toting food from the kitchen to the serving pantry were required to whistle to demonstrate that they weren't sampling the vittles.

Lives on the place: Has quarters on the premises.

Grace-and-favor house: Rent-free house. It comes with the job at 1600 Pennsylvania Avenue, Washington, D.C. A similar privilege is offered by the Mount Vernon Ladies' Association for the Union, Mount Vernon, Virginia, for the resident director of that attraction.

Wild Bill: Frontier name for a bed made by boring holes in two logs, connecting them with wooden rods, and covering it with sedge grass and hickory bark.

Shake down: An improvised bed, *circa* the Civil War.

Hooved up: Bowed up, as with a humpback trunk of the late 1880s.

Truck, household truck: Anything marauding Yankees could tote from Southern households in the Late Rebellion—silver, pots, pans, etc.

Plunder, house plunder: Furniture; household goods; bedding; odds and ends; luggage. An old New England word for "plunder" is "blenker."

Plunder room: A room for storage of seldom used clothing, household goods, luggage.

Trumpery: Trash; showy and worthless junk. It's akin to plunder and is stored in plunder rooms.

Fixments: Furnishings.

Front room: Company room; the best room; where the preacher sleeps.

Counterpins, coverlids: Counterpanes; bedspreads.

Soogans, sugans: Coarse blankets.

Latch pin: Safety pin. Also the wooden pin or peg over a door latch to keep it secured.

Bresh broom: A yard broom made of dogwood boughs.

Length of cloth: Enough cloth for a dress; some dresses don't have enough cloth to wad a shotgun.

Ordered cloth: Yard goods by way of a mail-order catalog.

Alamance cloth, Alamance plaids: A checked tan-and-blue fabric. Edwin M. Holt, of Alamance County, North Carolina, employed a French dyer and pioneered in the South, in 1853, in producing colored cotton cloth made on powered looms.

Butternut suit: A suit of homespun, butternut in color.

Linsey woolsey: Cloth of linen and wool.

Wash rag: Bath cloth.

Farthingale: Hooped petticoat.

Shimmy shirt: Chemise.

Comfortables: Knitted undergarments; drawers.

Rump sprung: A dress or trousers stretched out of shape across the rear.

Shift of clothes: A change of clothes.

T'other clothes: Sunday best.

Sunday-go-to-meeting clothes: Best bib and tucker.

Marryin' an' buryin' hat: One for special occasions.

Clean straw: Clean sheets.

Do up: Create; renovate; millinery shops do up hats for ladies.

Shake: A bonnet done up in wheat straw.

Slipper slide: Shoe horn.

Set a quilt together: Join in piecing a quilt.

Soap papers: Soap coupons. Soon after the Civil War, fifty soap papers were worth a sewing machine, sixty a Morris chair.

Tabernacled: Visited.

Battlin' board: A board in a stream on which clothes being laundered are beaten with a battle, a flat-sided bat or paddle.

> You sob 'em an' rensh 'em an' rub 'em in the trough, an' beat 'em with the battler on the battlin' bench.
> —An old quote

Throw out the wash: Count and assemble items to be laundered.

Borry the fone: Use a device installed for another's convenience.

Powerful handy: Convenient.

Ill convenient: Inconvenient.

Disfurnish: Deprive, as "I'm obliged to borry some sugar if it won't disfurnish you."

Swap work: Do manual labor for one who will, in turn, work for you.

Turn off work: A productive worker who can prime, or crop, two rows of tobacco at a time can turn off work; he's a good hand.

A good hand: One adapted for, inclined to, fitted for jobs of work; a good tobacco hand sits at the first table.

Cut out for: Some people aren't cut out for, or inclined to be, good hands because of laziness, indifference, or being all thumbs.

A-workin': A gathering of neighbors to peel logs, raise a barn, grub new ground, dig a well, chop wood—all-day jobs of working as a group for free.

Frolic: A party to celebrate the end of a-workin'. Frolics are associated with the maulin' or splittin' of logs, with bean stringin's, candy b'ilin's and pullin's, corn shuckin's, molasses b'ilin's, nut crackin's, quiltin's, peanut poppin's, and cotton-seed pickin's. Frolics also constitute mayhem, as in shootin's, cuttin's, eye-gougin's, hair-pullin's, tooth-loosenin's, rat-killin's, and other bucolic divertissements. You don't have to go far afield in the South to find a frolic or a fight. We are accommodating.

Granny frolic: A party of adult womenfolk to celebrate the birth of a grandchild.

Infare: A party attendant to a wedding, usually at the home of the groom's parents the day after the wedding, and sometimes followed by another at the home of the bride's parents. Hosts at infares spread themselves, or put on the dog, or do it up brown. Ms. Mary Boykin Chesnut, in *A Diary from Dixie,* described an infare held in Lincolnton, North Carolina, in the early days of the Civil War:

An "infare" means a table standing for days against all comers. At this one, they began to dine at two o'clock in the day, and dined on continuously. As soon as one relay were glutted, another came. Table or tables were constantly replenished. There were two tables in separate rooms; one for beef, bacon, turkeys, fowls, all meats and vegetables and the other for sweets. Everybody fared alike and all fared sumptuously. Without haste, without rest, on flowed the crowd of eaters. [Some soldiers said] that they had dined three times that day, and the last dinner was as good as the first.

Held his hind leg: Was best man at the wedding.

Crossroads kitchen sweat: Sukey jump; a frolic; a get-together for no particular reason except to socialize until all hours.

Hoedown: A riotous and lively dance combining the features of the jig and the reel. Ms. Chesnut described a hoedown as: "A Negro corn-shucking, heel-and-toe fling with a grapevine twist and all."

Dance straws: Dance a jig. The dance is a throwback to the sword dance of Highland Scots chieftains who, on the eve of battle centuries ago, danced in and out of a pattern of crossed broadswords as the piper played the "Gille Calum." Broomstraws now replace the swords of old.

Set-to: A confrontation.

Gee and haw together: What a couple in harmony do. In handling mules, "gee" is the command to turn right, "haw" left.

Was turned away: Was fired; was given his walking papers, or walking ticket.

Make time: Build up hours of employment.

Give time: Pay off, as when one is fired.

Uppin' stone, uppin' block: The step from which discreet ladies ascended to their sidesaddles, in days when women rode aside, or sidestraddle, or stradways, or side fashion.

In a-washin': In swimming.

Wrong-si-towt-ards: Wrong side out.

On the gander hill: Said of a husband who is close by his pregnant wife.

Minding his bees: What a husband on the gander hill is doing.

Pooched out: Distended, as a gravid goat; with a beer belly.

Kettle-bellied: Pot-bellied.

Snuffing: Putting pinches of snuff into the nostrils of an over-due woman to cause violent sneezing, thus inducing de-livery.

Horning: A method of snuffing—inserting snuff into the nos-trils by way of a paper cone.

Granny race: The hurryment of granny women—midwives—to help in childbirthing. Southern Appalachian granny women tried to outrace the baby and the doctor, if there was one on call, and have hot water on the stove and a chicken ready for frying after the main event.

Basket name: The pet name for an infant prior to christening.

Breast baby, sucking baby: A nursing baby.

Arm youngun: One toted in a mother's arms.

Lap baby: Too small to quit the lap; weaned but addicted to laps and sugar tits.

Knee baby: Next to the youngest, old and strong enough to play at a mother's knee.

Porch child: One sufficiently advanced to play unattended on a porch with protective devices, such as railings.

Yard child: Old enough to play in sand piles and eat dirt; also a term for a woods colt.

Set-along child: One that stays put as on a quilt at the end of a row of cotton.

Pickanniny: A small black child. Introduced by slaves from the West Indies, it was their way of pronouncing either Portu-guese *pequenino* or Spanish *pequeño niño*, terms they came upon in the West Indies or brought there from African use in Guinea, Stuart Berg Flexner says.

Trundlebed trash: Children, mildly censured.

It daddied itself: Said of a child that's the spittin' image of its pappy.

Hippin's, britchin's: Diapers.

Feathered out some: Grown some.

Send word in passing: Relay a verbal message by an informal route.

First passin': The next time somebody goes by here.

Roebuckers: False teeth. Probably from the catalog.

Snack house: Restaurant.

Quit home: Left bed and board.

Homing for: Homesick.

Back: Address a letter.

Acting pole, acting bar: A device suspended from a tree limb or a scaffold on which youngsters show off by skinning the cat.

Tail the cows: Hang on to cows' tails. A bucolic sport in which youngsters grab a-holt of tails of cows and are pulled along as the cows head for home and milking.

They let the gap down: Said of parents who've relinquished parental responsibilities and let their children roam free.

Jockey lot: Flea market. Originally an open space near the courthouse where, on Tuesdays of court week, horses were swapped. Horse traders were known as jockeys.

Rag shakin': Yard sale.

Nooning: Taking a short nap after a noon meal.

Shade up: Rest in the shade during the noonday sun.

Drop down, cool out: Same as above. While on his Southern tour in the spring of 1791, George Washington dropped down, shaded up, and cooled out under a live oak tree that remains standing today, close by U. S. Highway 17 at Hampstead, North Carolina.

Grabble: Find by working the fingers, as in recovering sweet taters from a hill of same, and catching trout in mountain pools. At dinner during the War of the Second Rebellion, Colonel James Chesnut of South Carolina observed the dirty hands of Henry Persy Brewster, a South Carolinian who had moved to Texas, had been Sam Houston's secretary and Attorney General of the Republic of Texas, had helped organize the Confederate Postal Service, and now was on the staff of General John B. Hood. Colonel Chesnut, according to his wife, said to Brewster, "My dear fellow, if you have such an aversion to water, why not grabble in a little clean sand?"

Dingle berries, dill berries, fartleberries: Small wads of fecal and seminal deposits in the hair of the anus and the female pudendum.

Strikin' paper: Toilet paper.

Setter: Buttocks.

Cucumbers: Testicles.

Go to Congress: Answer a call of nature in bosky dell facilities. A reflection on the bad repute of the Confederate Congress of 1863. It made few positive contributions to the war effort, its members posturing, quarreling, boozing, and creating shameful scenes resulting from an exaggerated sense of honor and a willingness to commit mayhem.

Inspect timber, go to the bushes: Same as above.

Make a branch: Urinate al fresco.

See how high the moon is: Same as above.

Doff the kidneys: Textile-worker term for urinating.

Trash, morning job, morning toilet: Euphemisms for handling the first of the day's calls of nature.

Hockey, doodley: Euphemisms foisted on the droopy drawers set, relating to the above.

Thunder mug: Chamber pot; slop jar.

Chamber lye: Urine deposited in thunder mugs. To produce saltpeter—potassium nitrate, niter—for the manufacture of explosives, ordnance people in the Confederate government were resourceful. They leached the soil from smokehouses, stables, and caves, for instance, to utilize nitrogenous refuse. Particularly ingenious was the agent who, on October 1, 1863, ran this advertisement in the Selma (Alabama) *Sentinel:*

> The Ladies of Selma are respectfully requested to preserve all their chamber lye collected about their premises, for the purpose of making "Nitre." Wagons, with barrels, will be sent around for it by the subscriber.
> (Signed) JOHN HARROLSON.
> Agent of Nitre and Mining Bureau.

The advertisement attracted the attention of a Southern poet whose name has been lost to history but who left this to posterity:

REBEL GUNPOWDER

John Harrolson! John Harrolson!
You are a funny creature;
You've given to this cruel war

39

A new and curious feature.
You'd have us think while ev'ry man
   Is bound to be a fighter,
The women, (bless the pretty dears,)
   Should be put to making nitre.

John Harrolson! John Harrolson!
   How could you get the notion
To send your barrels 'round the town
   To gather up the lotion?
We think the girls do work enough
   In making love and kissing.
But you'll now put the pretty dears
   To patriotic pissing!

John Harrolson! John Harrolson!
   Could you not invent a meter,
Or some less immodest mode
Of making our salt-petre?
   The thing, it is so queer, you know—
   Gunpowder, like the crankey—
That when the lady lifts her shift
   She shoots a bloody Yankee.

John Harrolson! John Harrolson!
   What 'ere was your intention,
You've made another contraband
   Of things we hate to mention.
What good will all our fighting do,
   If Yankees search Venus's mountains,
And confiscate and carry off
   These Southern nitre fountains!

These lines crossed the lines and in time there came this response from the Yankee side:

REBEL GUNPOWDER

John Harrolson! John Harrolson!
We've read in song and story

How women's tears through all the years
   Have moistened fields of glory.
But never was it told before
   Amid such scenes of slaughter
Your Southern beauties dried their tears
   And went to making water.

No wonder that your boys are brave.
   Who couldn't be a fighter
If every time he fired his gun,
   He used his sweetheart's nitre;
And vice-versa, what would make
   A Yankee sadder
Than dodging bullets fired
   From a pretty woman's bladder?

They say there was a subtle smell
   That lingered in the powder,
And as the smoke grew thicker
   And the din of battle louder,
That there was found
   To this compound,
One serious objection.
   No soldier could sniff it
Without having an erection.

Bawdy items pertaining to the Civil War are hard to come by. We thank James O. Breeden and Tom Broadfoot for bringing this paramount contribution to the light of day.

Use: Urinate; defecate, as "That houn' dog used in the baby's pallet."

Grass widow: One widowed by divorce.

Sod widow: One widowed by death.

Fore-parents: Forefathers.

Bucking: Two people swinging another's rear against a tree or post; the paddling one gets after losing a rasslin' match.

Fiddlin', sawin': A trick to entice fishing worms to the surface by driving a stake in the ground and fiddlin', or sawin', on it with an iron bar or a stone; it's more heard of than done.

Sleep heads and tails: Crowd into a bed.

Nesting: Staying; making one's self at home.

Joggle board, joggling board, jinky board, janky board: A recreational device. Joggle boards are thick boards with give, or bounce, suspended between two uprights and upon which children, mostly, bounce; they flourish best under shade trees on large lawns and on big porches.

# Notes on Meanness, Mayhem, and Other Virtues

*He was settin' in the front room, and when I walked in he didn't say nothin', just whipped out his pistol and snapped the hammer down on an empty chamber.*

*I said, "I don't want no trouble," but all he done was pull the hammer down on another empty chamber. By that time I was gettin' kinda nervous, of course, so I yanked out my pistol and I shot him.*

*If that taught me anything, it were never to let no man get the draw on me again.*

—John Wright, a peace officer in
Letcher County, Kentucky

He's mean enough to steal cracklin's from his mammy's fat gourd: He'd steal anything that ain't too hot or too heavy to tote. Cracklin's are what are left when lard is rendered in pork processing. A fat gourd is a receptacle for storing cracklin's and kitchen grease for cooking and for making lye soap.

He'd steal a chaw of tobacco out of your mouth if you yawned.

He'd steal flies from a blind spider.

He's mean as gar broth and ashes: He's mean as a junkyard dog. Borrowed and passed along by Herb Caen: "Neither rain nor sleet nor dead of night nor a junkyard dog nor woman scorned can stay these courageous reporters from the incisive and exact exercise of their awesome responsibility to tell it like it is. Mostly."

He's mean enough to burn bresh of a Sunday: He's so mean a rattlesnake struck him five times and died.

He'd fight a circ'l saw: He'd tear up an anvil; he'd fight a steam sawmill.

He's tough as a boot: He's tough as whitleather.

He could whip a camp meetin' of wildcats: He'd knock you sky west and crooked and four ways from Sunday.'

Tough as a lightard knot: Tough enough to raise hell and put a chunk under it. Lightard (lightwood) knots come from pine stumps in which rosin has settled; they are extremely hard and difficult to cut.

Rough as a cob: Abrasive; raspy. Anyone using corn cobs in morning jobs understands who somebody rough as a cob is—somebody you'd want on your side in a fight and somebody you'd rather not meet in a dark alley.

Fighty-fied: Inclined to fight; has a short fuse; easily angered.

His snuff's too strong: Said of someone who's hot under the collar.

44

Techous, touchous: Sensitive as an eyeball; has a short fuse; is quick to become offended.

Ringy: Tough; riled up; acts smart-ass, as in "Don' you go gittin' ringy with me now, you heah me?"

Has his tail over the dashboard: He's ringy.

High-tempered: Said of one who easily becomes ill as a hornet.

Blow a gasket: Exhibit a quick temper tantrum, as one who got up on the wrong side of the bed.

Make the cap fly: Explode in sudden anger. From moonshiner's argot: Caps on whiskey stills blow off when unwary or unskilled operators "push it too fast." When they apply too much heat to the mash being converted into booze, the pressure blows the cap off the still pot.

Mad as fire: Displays a fiery temper, sparks flying.

Mad as a settin' hen: Angry and puffed up.

Mad enough to spit tacks: Spittin' mad; about to bust a b'iler.

Mad enough to chew nails an' spit rivets: B'ilin' mad.

Serious mad: Downright fire-eatin', ass-chewin' mad.

Fernlin' mad: Fire-spittin', arm-wavin', dish-throwin' mad. Fernlin' mad women send cats through cat holes, children to hiding behind chimneys, neighbors to windows, and strong men to strong drink. Fernlin' mad women resemble tornadoes in featherbed factories, only more so—sort of like a windmill gone bad.

Upscuddle: A quarrel.

Played thunder: Played hell; erred, and no two ways about it.

Puggle: Punch; annoy, as one pokes at varmints in hollow gum logs.

Contrary: Antagonize; contradict.

Banter: Challenge; dare; defy.

Like all wrath: Vehement.

Hassle, crowd: Pertains to semi-hostile encounter; "don't hassle him" means "get off his back—leave him be." When a dog hassles he breathes noisily and pants with his tongue hanging loose and long.

Dallas special: A pocket knife with a blade longer than legal.

Arkansas toothpick: A sheath knife eighteen inches long, double-edged and with a fine point. Rezin Pleasant Bowie, brother of Jim Bowie of Alamo fame, is credited with its invention in Washington, Arkansas. Soldiers of the 3rd Arkansas toted the long blades in battles of the Lost Cause.

Crab apple switch: A spring-bladed knife.

Stob: Stab; drive a knife into somebody or something. In Southern precincts hardly anyone is "stabbed." Rather, he's "stobbed." One takes a stab at, or a try at, a job of work. But when you stob somebody it's real business and for keeps.

Bad-mouth, lay a slur, talk trash: "I'm gonna stomp a mudhole in you if you don't quit talkin' trash about me."

Harm words: Words used in bad-mouthin'.

Scandalize his name: Put the bad mouth on him.

A-squanderin' off: Exchanging hard words.

Back cuss: Return the compliment; give it back to the one who first cussed you.

Bawl out: Rebuke in heated terms; give one down the country; upbraid.

Bless out, cuss out, dress down: Same as above.

Rarr: An argument.

Sass: Back talk; back jaw; lip; insolent dialogue.

Ill word: One spoken in anger.

Think hard of: Speak ill or unkindly of another.

Hold a hard spirit: Same as above.

Pass some words: Quarrel, as "They commenced to pass some words an' then they fell in an' fit."

Fit: Fought; when they fell in an' fit, they fout.

Stir-up: A dust-up; a dispute of a nonverbal sort.

Use: Employ with malice aforethought, as "I'll use this here ax on his noggin."

Bulldoze, bulldose: To deliver a severe castigation; to flog; to intimidate by unlawful and violent means; to bully. Bulldosing was originally the method of an association of Negroes in Louisiana, the Union Rights Stop League, formed to insure by strong measures the success of an election. If any member was suspected of supporting the Democratic ticket he was warned; if he failed to fall in line he was flogged with a bull whip. If he hadn't yet gotten the message, he was shot.

Meet at the store: Coal mine talk for arranging a fracas. Belligerents can't have at each other in a mine's depths, but they can tangle later at a common meeting ground, such as the company store.

Lay one on him: Lay him out; best him in physical or verbal exchange. To "lay out" also means to prepare someone for burial.

Give 'em Jessie: Punish; castigate. "We'll give 'em Jessie" was one of half a dozen campaign songs in honor of Jessie Benton Fremont, child bride of John C. Fremont, and used in her husband's campaign against James Buchanan for president in 1856.

Ride a-bug huntin': Chastise. Originally, rub someone's nose in dirt.

Raise a breeze: Create excitement.

Egg on: Incite.

Fix his clock: Fix his little red wagon; take him down a peg.

Fix his flint: Same as above.

Tan: Thrash, as "I'll tan yore hide till it won't hold shucks."

Hang his hide on a fence: Whip him for all to see.

Grab where the hair is short: Assault verbally in debate or argument and make a telling point.

Mix his wool: Settle his hash; whip him in a fight.

Clean his plow: Tell him off; give him what for; thrash him.

Sharpen his hoe: Same as above.

Cold cock: Relieve one of consciousness.

Ruction, ruckus, rookus: A fray; a fight.

They tore up some corn rows: They had a knock-down and drag-out.

Frail: Beat the daylights out of the opposition.

Raise five dollars worth of hell: Enjoy high times and misdemeanors in a Saturday-night town.

Frap, frop: Strike with intent to gain attention or maim.

A right good lick: A solid blow; a good effort.

Mislick: A misdirected blow.

Haul off: Take strong action, as in "I hauled off an' cold-cocked him."

Throw up to, throw off on: Low-rate; lay a slur; precise definition of one's ancestry or environment can induce umbrage of the most violent sort.

Feather up to: Show fight; itch for a showdown. When you feather up you cast a reflection on the old days, when bows and arrows were the ultimate weapon—when you drove an arrow into a body all the way to the feathers at the other end of the shaft.

Feathers up, hackles up, dander up: A little bit angry; belligerently on guard. Cockfighting is the source of "feathers up" and "hackles up."

Throw a fit: Some overly angry and/or spoiled people manage to contrive duck and conniption fits, or unseemly displays of temper and bad manners.

Swarpin': Thrashing around, as in "When he gits a few drinks in him, he starts swarpin' about."

Get taken to the woodshed: Get taken to the place where you get a hiding; where somebody lays one on you with a switch of hickory or peach. The punishment is compounded when the victim must provide an acceptable weapon.

Put the bud to you: Give you a switching. A dose of hickory oil is a switching with a hickory switch; a dose of strop oil is applied with a razor strap or a leather belt.

You'll ketch it: You're in for it; you'll be punished.

Swinge: What's coming to you in the switching department.

Bush shot: A shot taken by irresponsible hunters, most often with rifles, at most anything in woods and fields that moves. Fatalities and fights often result from such indifferent sportsmanship.

Bring to the lick log: Force the opposition to accept your way of thinking; face up to an unpleasant duty fairly and squarely. A lick log is a fallen tree trunk with notches cut in it to hold salt for cattle to lick.

Bring to taw: Bring to task; teach one a lesson.

Split the biscuit and butter it: Prevail in an argument or fight.

Havin' the up-ards: Same as above.

Put the feet to the fire: Force a decision.

Made: Intimidated, as in "He made at me with a razor an' I pulled my thirty-eight an' was thow'in' down on 'im when somebody flang a cheer at the lantun." When someone flang a cheer at the lantun, he threw a chair and knocked over the lantern, leaving the place without light and maybe setting the place on fire. At any rate, he changed the direction of the action in progress.

Call for calf rope: Surrender; holler uncle; as the horny possum said to the accommodating lady skunk: "I've enjoyed about as much of this as I can stand."

# Something to See, I'm A-Tellin' You

*Pat [Harrison] can cross a creek on a slick log, in the rain, with a live eel in his hands, a bucket of water balanced on his head, and never spill a drop nor miss a step.*

> —James K. Vardaman of
> Mississippi, in a campaign
> against Harrison for the U. S.
> Senate in 1918

Sockdologer: Something exceptional or overwhelming, as Dolly Parton's rib cage. "Sockdologer" is from the frontier vocabulary of moren a century ago. It seems to be combination of *sock*, meaning "a strong blow," and *dolager*, a corruption of doxology. Thus it means anything truly decisive—the ultimate.

51

That beats hens a-pacin': Observation made of a sexy woman's gait, manner, or dress.

That beats cock-fighting: Something that is fourteen-karat, thirty-second-degree, triple-distilled.

Hen waller jostle: A lively movement in place, starting from the bottom and moving up. From the way a hen shakes all over in a dust bath.

Loose as a goose: Limp as a dishrag. The imagery relates to the bowel movements of a goose.

Fast bean-polin' up: Gwine tuh duh j'ists (growing so fast he's about to reach the joists, the beams that support the ceiling above).

So cross-eyed she could look at her own head.

Ragged-assed: Unkempt.

Decked up, diked out, tricked out: Dressed fit to kill; dressed to the nines.

Drunk an' dressed up: Uncomfortable while dressed to the nines in one's best bib and tucker. To be dressed up drunk is to be dressed to excess.

Give me a fly-flapper and I'll help you kill it: Opinion registered of an outlandish hairdo, dress, or get-up.

Drunk as Cooter Brown: Someone who can't hit the ground with his hat in three throws.

Been hit in the face with a bag full of nickels, or a wet squirrel: So ugly he has to sneak up on a glass of water to get a drink.

Hard-favored: A face to stop a clock.

Good-countenanced: Opposite of hard-favored.

He's so ugly he has to slap himself to sleep: He'd gag a maggot.

He's so ugly his mother had to borrow a baby to take to church: He's so hard-favored they had to tie a pork chop around his neck so the dog would play with him.

He'd frighten a horse from his oats: He's ugly as hell's old shavin' hoss. A shavin' hoss is a device used in riving shingles, or shakes.

He's so ugly he could turn a train down a dirt road: He's ugly as a forty-mile road.

Ugly as a stump full of spiders: Ugly as a mud fence staked and ridered with tadpoles. Horizontal members in a rail fence are supported and heightened by rails called stakes and riders.

He's so ugly no fly'd ever land on him: He's like something the cat drug in and the dog wouldn't eat.

Looks like he's been chewin' tobacco and spittin' in the wind: He's ill-favored; ugly as sin; ugly as homemade soap; homely enough to curdle milk.

She's so ugly the tide wouldn't take her out: Stomp-down ugly.

He looks like he's been sortin' wildcats: He looks as raw as he'd been tapped for turpentine.

He looks like the hindquarters of bad luck: He could back a dog off a meat truck.

He had a face that would've soured buttermilk: When he was a baby he was so ugly they fed him with a slingshot.

No fly ever lit on her: She's immaculate.

As pretty as the seven stars in Ellen's yard: As pretty as the constellation Orion. These stars were unusually bright and exciting to see in the late 1870s.

You'd walk her down to the front row at the revival meeting: She's pretty as a speckled puppy; she's the prettiest woman that ever stood in shoe leather; she's the whipped cream on the pie.

She's so fat you couldn't tell which wrinkle she'd open to talk: She's fleshy.

She's so fat that if she had to haul ass she'd have to make two trips: Same as above.

Heavier than a ton of lard in a bucket of molasses: Big as a bale of cotton.

Fat as a mullet: Fat as a sausage salesman at a county fair.

Throddy: Well rounded; plump; chuffy.

Low set and on the heavy side: Stocky; built from the ground up.

Too big for a man and not big enough for a horse: Of an awkward size.

Poor as a snake: So thin she could wash in a gun barrel.

If she stuck her tongue out she'd look like a zipper: Skinny.

If she drank a Cherry Smash she'd look like a thermometer: Same as above.

Thin as a cake of lye soap after a week's washing: Thin as a May shad in spawning season.

Two ax handles across: Opposite of above.

Shingle-butted: Slab-assed; with flat buttocks. Slabs are outside pieces sawed from logs, with a knot protruding here and there.

She's got pones on her hips: Her buttocks are lumpy.

Born short and slapped down flat: Undersized.

High-rumpted: Long of legs, short of body.

Dry grin: The forced smile of one hacked, teased, or embarrassed.

Narrow between the eyes: Not to be trusted.

Bread jerker: Adam's apple; goozle; the projection formed by the thyroid cartilage in the neck.

Stinks like cyarn: Stinks like carrion.

Rank: Smells high; the odor of one who wears clothing for six thousand miles without changing, or whose breath smells like he chewed his socks.

Naked as a scraped hog: Bare-assed naked.

Start nekkid, stark naked: Naked as a jaybird. Start is from the Anglo-Saxon "steort," meaning tail.

His face is lit up like a new saloon: He's bright-eyed and bushy-tailed.

His face was all plowed up: His face was creased and wrinkled.

His nose was drippin' like a ash hopper: Dripping in a steady dribble. An ash hopper is a trough in which wood ashes from fireplaces and cookstoves are stored. Water is poured over them and potash is leached out in a moderate and steady stream and used with kitchen grease to make lye soap.

Never saw the beat of it, never saw the like of it: You've seen something you sho' nuff never laid eyes on previously.

Caution, a: Something out of the ordinary.

Put on the dog, strut your stuff: Show off; show off with a gaited horse reined up tight and hitched to a rubber-tired buggy.

# Man's Best Friend
## and Assorted Associates

When W. Kerr Scott campaigned to become Governor of North Carolina he appealed strongest to voters whose roots were in the soil. "Branchhead boys," he called them, farmers and townspeople who knew the bust of day, coffee that's saucered and blowed, folks who made a good stagger at honest toil and plowed to the end of the row. Scott campaigned to get the farmer out of the mud, he said, so farm families could get to church and farm children to school.

Soon after taking office he astonished the state by proposing a $200,000,000 bond issue, big money in 1949, for a secondary road program. He would pave farm-to-market roads in each of the 100 counties. The bonds would be amortised by a gasoline tax. The proposal was revolutionary, the reaction mixed. Debate was heated and families were split and friendships were jeopardized.

In this seething setting a branchhead boy in Montgomery County came one day to the crossroads store where he traded and loafed. Some of his peers sat about the wood stove and *spat in the spit box and berated Governor Scott and deplored the bond issue and the tax levy. They were in ferment.*

*"Well," one of the group said, taunting the newcomer, "what do you think of your man Scott now?"*

*Shifting his cud and eyeballing his questioner, the branch-head boy replied:*

*"Anything my dog trees, I'll eat."*

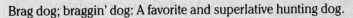

Brag dog; braggin' dog: A favorite and superlative hunting dog.

Plan'ation dog: A dog to keep cows and hogs out of corn, peanut, and bean fields.

Ketch dog: A dog to help round up stock.

Start dog: An experienced brag dog depended on to pick up a fox trail at the start of a night hunt.

Pot licker, grade dog: A hunting dog without claim to registration papers.

Suck-egg dog: An epithet, as in "mean as a suck-egg dog."

Going to the bow-wows: Going to the dogs.

A dog's chance: None whatever.

Proud as a dog with two tails: Fine as dollar cotton.

Proud as a dog with a hemstitched tail: Same as above.

Lazy as Hall's dog: He leaned against a fence to bark.

Long as Marion's dog: The dog that Marion Miller saw close to a hainted house at midnight was twelve feet long.

That dog won't hunt, that cock won't fight: The hell you say; it ain't practical; my hind foot; you're trying to sell me a bill of goods; I won't buy that excuse; that won't wash; in a pig's eye; you're pissin' on my leg.

Stretched out: A bird dog straining to extend himself while holding a point.

Chop-tongued: A dog with a short yelp, a staccato bark, instead of a full, round, bell-like voice, when hot on a trail. Dogs trail and run foxes; when trailing, the scent is cold and the music erratic. When running, the fox is up and away and the hounds are in full cry.

Pretty mouth, sweet mouth: What a dog in good voice has when he opens, or bays, or begins to mouth on a hunt.

Bawl, squall: A long and mournful howl.

Tight-mouthed: Doesn't bark much.

Free tonguer; open dog: Barks muchly.

Meat dog: Barks only when he has treed the coon.

Close dog: A beagle that stays near the rabbit's trail.

Blanket back: A black and tan beagle.

Tree: To bark and hit a tree with front paws, indicating that a coon is up the tree.

Slick tree: No coon here.

Gone coon; gone goose: Said of someone hopelessly lost.

We have treed the coon: Eureka; we have found the culprit; we have found the quarry; we found where they hid the case of Canadian Club.

Cut a hog: Make a mess of things.

Bull-proof and pig-tight: Secure; impregnable.

Shoot me for a billy goat: Well I'll be damned; I'll be dipped in shit.

Joree: A red-eyed towhee. Governor Marvin Griffin of Georgia described reporters who irritated him as "jorees." "Small birds," he said, "always scratching around in dirt.

Pojo, poor joe: A blue heron.

Peep frogs: Spring peepers. These noisy frogs erupting from the mud of hibernation are pinklewinks on Martha's Vineyard and pinkwinks on Cape Cod. Most everywhere they are voices of Spring.

Chiggers: Red bugs.

Gallinipper: An insect pest resembling a mosquito, but bigger and slower.

Flinder: Butterfly; moth.

Whistle pig: Groundhog.

Gnat ball: A dense swarm of gnats or other small flying insects.

Snake doctors, snake feeders, skeeter hawks: Dragonflies.

Talk turkey: Discuss something flat out.

Bad to kick: Apt to kick, as an ill-natured cow or horse.

Stone horse: A stud.

Bottom: Endurance in a horse, as "That there red horse there's got good bottom."

Marsh tacky: Small horses of the sea islands of Virginia, North Carolina, South Carolina, and Georgia.

"He's a stone horse."
"A stud?"

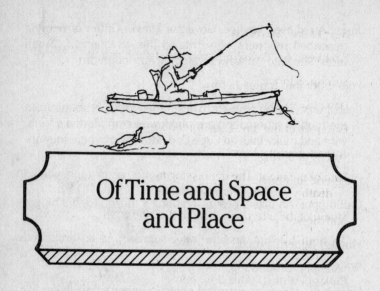

# Of Time and Space and Place

*There are more rivers and less water, and more mines and less ore, and you can see farther and see less than in any damned country in the world.*

— *Texas, as seen by "Marse Henry" Watterson of Kentucky*

From kin to cain't, from kin see to cain't see: From before first light to good dark.

Day clean to first dark: A tad shorter than the above.

Peep of day, morngloam: When the first streaks of dawn appear.

Comin' day, comin' light: Same as above.

# Of Time and Space and Place

Bust of day: Daybreak.

First light, fus day: When you can distinguish the horizon.

Sun up: Sunrise.

Day clean: Good day; good daylight; broad daylight.

Fore part of the day: Early forenoon.

Turn of the sun: Noon.

Turn of the night: The depressing middle of the night when the deathly sick are supposed to die.

Shank of the afternoon: Late in the afternoon.

An hour by sun: An hour after sunrise and an hour before sunset.

Pink of evening; pinked in: Sunset.

Edge of dark: Twilight.

Day down, daylight down: First dark; when you can't distinguish the horizon.

Evening: Often regarded as afternoon.

Early candle lighting: Early evening.

Gray as Aunt Rhody's goose: Dusky dark; dusty dark.

As soon as it's dark in the churn: That's when you go to bed with the chickens to get up with the rooster.

Good dark: Dark as three feet up a bull's ass.

Dark of the moon, waste of the moon, down side of the moon, shrink of the moon: When the moon is waning, or decreasing. This is the time to plant root crops such as potatoes, turnips, rutabagas. Shingles won't curl as they dry if rived now, and lye soap will thicken better if made now. Little or no dirt is left over when graves are filled on the shrink of the moon, and apples picked now will keep longer, for any bruises on them will shrink and dry up rather than rot.

Light of the moon, coming up of the moon: When the moon is waxing, growing, fattening, increasing. Now is the time to plant top crops, those producing their yield above ground, such as squash, garden peas, butterbeans. Distillers of moonshine whiskey and apple brandy know that on a growing moon the mash and the cider pimper, or ferment, work faster.

Now, too, is the time to pick feathers from geese—one *picks* feathers but *plucks* hairs—for the roots of the quills grow deeper as the moon ages, and on the new moon there is less bleeding and tearing of skin.

New of the moon: New moon.

Dark moon: The interval between new moon and old.

Of a morning, of an evening: Times of day, as "Of a mornin' he's got a paper route, an' of an evenin' he works at the pitcher show."

Church-goin' bell: The last bell, and if you're late you'll have to sit in the front pew.

Turn-out bell: It's time to turn out, to return to work.

The twelve borrowing days of April: When spring cleaning starts. In Southern folklore, old cows celebrate at the end of March on having survived the winter. But March borrows a dozen days from April and claims the cows anyway.

Borned days: Whole life; whole put together, as "Nevuh in my borned days did I evuh heah tell such."

Handful days: Busy days, as in harvest time.

Struttin' an' gobblin' time: Early spring; when one comes of age; a time for lovin'.

Sap-risin' time: Same as above.

Railroad time: Correct time. You can't set your watch by television times.

Endurin' time: An indefinite measure, as "He slep' the whole endurin' time an' woke up hongry's a b'ar."

Most any time now: About now, as in "The horse trough will freeze over most any time now."

Odd come shorts: An indefinite period; an odd moment.

Short times: Between times of gainful employment.

Height of the time: Most of the time.

Pull time: Serve a prison term.

Pass some time, pass the time of day, pass a chat: A neighborly gesture involving brief conversation.

Big meeting time: The hottest months of summer when planting and cultivating have ended and crops laid by; farmers put their futures in the lap of the Lord and join their families in rural churches for a week of religious services. This time and the next three refer to gentler times—before mechanization and windshield farmers—when crops were mainly corn, cotton, and tobacco, and cultivation was accomplished by a man, a mule, and a plow.

Lay-by time: Usually from the Fourth of July to Labor Day; crop cultivation has about run its course, the last furrows have been busted, and there is a little slack before it's time to pull corn and pick cotton; now is time for fishing and for protracted meetings with dinner on the grounds.

Packin' time: Cotton ginning time. Cotton is packed in bales at cotton gins.

Bustin'-out-the-middles time: When furrows are plowed to uproot weeds and to loosen soil to let the rain soak in.

Green shuck time: Time for tender roas'n' ears.

Barefoot weather: Summer.

Days of bright blue weather: Early fall; late September and early October.

Amber days: Indian Summer, when leaves begin to turn and the sun is warm as an old blanket.

Chestnut time: Fall.

Fodder pullin' time: Late fall.

Bull bat time: Time for a drink; the sun's below the yardarm; it's milkin' time; it's five o'clock somewhere.

> The martins build in boxes,
> The foxes den in holes.
> The sarpints crawl in rockses,
> The earth's the home of moles.
> Cock-a-doodle do, hit's movin',
> An' dram-time's come again.
> —An old refrain

As long as Pat stayed in the army: No time a-tall.

Quicker'n a cat can lick his ass: Lickety-split.

Quick as double-geared lightning: Same as above.

Soon: Early, as "I'll be there soon in the mornin'."

A wagon greasing: The distance between places, judged by how long a time between greasings of the wagon wheels.

Right smart; right good: A span of time and right indefinite; an amount, also indefinite, as in "We cut a right smart mess of stovewood."

Right on: Didn't stop, as "She hollered an' he went right on."

Whip stitch: A brief interval.

Spell: An indefinite period—brief, extensive, or right square in between—depending on the situation.

Whole put together: Lifetime.

Between hay and grass: Between boyhood and manhood; too late for one thing, too early for another.

Between whiles: Meantime.

Near 'bout: Almost; near to, as "She near 'bout died a-laughin'."

Mighty nigh: Near at hand; near 'bout could, as "The moon was mighty nigh—it was so bright you could mighty nigh pick up a pin almost."

Plum' nelly: Plumb nearly; almost. In Dade County, Georgia's northwesternmost country, is Plum Nelly—"plum' out of Tennessee and nelly out of Georgia"—a craft center noted for its annual "clothes line" art show.

Purt near; pretty near: Close.

Nigher: Nearer.

Nigh ways; Shortcuts across the countryside.

In a little of: Almost; damned near; near 'bout; like to of.

Within a lash: Within the blinking of an eye.

Within a peg: Within an inch; a moment, as in "She was within a peg of dying." From an old method of measuring yard-goods on a country store countertop: one peg equals one inch.

Right smack dab: A particular and definite location; squarely, as in "That cat stole in an' stooled right smack dab in the solid middle of Bascom Bignall Benehan's spankin' bran'-new drugget."

Holus-bolus: All in a lump.

Till there's enough frost in hell to kill snap beans: To the end of time.

Till the last pea is out of the pot: To the very last.

In the last of pea time: In declining years.

Slow as Moses: Not hasty; a contraction of "slow as molasses." Moses was no slouch at taking his own sweet time. He wandered in the wilderness, day and night and on weekends, for forty years.

Slow as seven-year itch and seven years behind scratchin': Slow as coal tar running uphill backwards; he's so slow he's the right feller to send for the doctor if the devil was sick.

Mudge: Move slowly; work in a leisurely fashion.

Mosey: Drift off, afoot, without hurry; move along.

Cooter around: Knock about; mosey.

Shammuck, shammick: Walk in a slouchy, unsteady manner.

He'd walk the legs off a dead mule: Opposite of above.

Still priming lugs: Lagging; still at the drawing board. The term is from tobacco harvesting: Lugs are bottom leaves, first to ripen, first to be removed from the stalk.

Take a slack: Slow down; take a break; take a blow; let the mules rest.

Slacked: Slowed, as of a flower that's "growed from thuh fus an' ain't slacked yit."

Slack: One holds a tight rein or gives slack in handling fish, animals, people. In the War for Southern Independence, Marse Robert gave Jeb Stuart too much slack. Stuart chased after a Yankee wagon train, neglecting his scouting assignment, and Lee thus was unprepared for what awaited him at Gettysburg.

Left out: Checked out; departed, as "She left out of here on the shoo-fly."

Get-go: The start; the beginning, as in "These are hard-core fans who've been with this band since the get-go."

Run-ago: A running jump, as in "He took a run-ago an' cleared that there rail fence there an' hit the groun' a-runnin'."

Fixin' for high ridin': Preparing for a hurried departure.

Hump: Hurry; get a move on; get in the go long, as "You better get a hump on or we won't finish a-fore it clouds up an' rains."

Sweepin' trot: In a big hurry.

Coat tails a-poppin': In an angry hurry.

With every foot up an' toenails draggin': Hurrying as fast as a pullet anticipating her first egg.

Flag your kite: Hit the breeze; get a hump on.

Hurryment: Confusion; like fighting fire.

Like a two-forty trot: Making good time. The pace required for a horse to trot a mile in two minutes, forty seconds. When the Standardbred stud book was established, any horse listed had to make the mile in at least two-thirty.

Skedaddle: Git up an' dust; get your ass over the dashboard and go. Skedaddle was used by troops on both sides in the Civil War to describe precipitous departure of the opposition from a fray. Ms. Chesnut said the word was like General Nathan Bedford Forrest's words of command: "In place of 'Boots and Saddles' played by the trumpet, he says; 'Git ready to git! Git!'" Slaveholders often used the term in advertising for runaways.

Light a shuck, light a rag: Make haste. From matchless days when neighbors borrowed fire from one another. To tote borrowed fire, corn shucks and rags were ignited, and to move such fire from one place to another one had to make tracks with celerity. Often chunks of smoldering wood were borrowed for repayment in kind.

He went like he was taking a shovel full of fire: He lit out.

He was burning shucks: Same as above.

Come to borry fire: No time to tarry.

Hell bent for election, like a big-assed bird: When one tore out, or racked out, or balled the jack, or was callihootin', or moved in a hurry.

Sift dirt: Move into high gear; high-tail it.

Put the hammer down, shower down: Same as above. To take the rough edges off a horse, you "let the hammer down."

Haul buggy, light out for, cut out for: Leave hurriedly; be like Moody's goose.

Pull freight for the tules: Run for cover; head for tall timber; take to the bushes; take to the brush; make tracks; go to the le'ward; hit the grit. "Tules" are bullrushes growing on overflowed land.

Break down timber: Same as above.

Run like a turpentined dog: It's Katy bar the door and no time to stop for wood, water, or coal.

Join the bird gang: Flee; jump to safety. Railroad talk for jumping from an overturning car or engine.

Slope: Elope; escape, run away.

Get up a head of steam: Begin something with vigor; talk volubly.

They let the gap down: The situation wherein you can't cross the road because of too much oncoming traffic.

Somebody opened the gate: Same as above.

Texas fever: An urge to settle in Texas, beginning in the 1820s when hundreds of Americans answered Mexico's offer of cheap land.

Gone for Texas, sloped for Texas: Skipped out just ahead of the sheriff or an incipient father-in-law and headed for Texas.

"You all can go to hell an' I'm a-goin' to Texas," said Davy Crockett, frontiersman and political figure, on leaving Tennessee after having been defeated by Andrew Jackson's followers for a third term in Congress. He died a year later, in 1836, in the Alamo.

When southeastern sheriffs failed to find men cited on their wanted lists, they usually entered in their records "G. T. T."—gone to Texas. Some folks who left voluntarily often left the initials on their doorways. In the antebellum South, abandoned cotton lands, worn out and eroded, were known as "gone-to-Texas" farms.

Absquatulate: Abscond; decamp.

Slipped the bridle: Absconded.

Piss on the far an' call the dogs: Let's get the hell out of here.

Water up the wagon wheels: Prepare to travel. From days when one soaked dry wagon wheels in streams and ponds so that the spokes would swell tight into hubs and felloes, or fellies.

Let's put the chairs in the wagon: It's time to leave out and head for home.

Gone: Disappeared, as "I don' know how come that play purty got gone."

Over to: Gone to, as "Alida's over to Salter Path."

Whistling up a gum tree: Just whistling "Dixie"; wasting time and effort.

As long as geese go barefooted: Forever.

As long as Tom Johnson's new ground: A long and narrow strip of farmland cleared by an eccentric.

Fresh out of: It was just now that you ran out of something or other.

D'rectly: An indefinite but usually short span of time.

Will tend to it d'rectly: When damned good and ready.

We'll be along d'rectly: Don't believe it if the promise comes from a courtin' couple on a moonlit beach.

Not commonly: Not often; infrequently.

Fixin' to: About to; on the point of, as "She's jus fixin' to fix supper on the cookstove." Charles Dickens was fascinated by our use of the word "fix." In his *American Notes,* a report on his travels in 1842, he wrote:

> There are few words which perform such various duties as this word "fix." It is the Caleb Quotem of the American vocabulary. You call upon a gentleman in a country town, and his help informs you that he is "fixing himself" just now, but will be down directly; by which you understand that he is dressing. You inquire, on board a steamboat, of a fellow-passenger, whether breakfast will be ready soon, and he tells you he should think so, for, when he was last below, they were "fixing the tables," in other words, laying the cloth. You beg a porter to collect your luggage, and he entreats you not to be uneasy, for he'll "fix it presently:" if you complain of an indisposition, you are advised to have recourse in Doctor So-and-so, who will "fix" you in no time.

Up over in back: Beyond another mountain.

In back of: Behind.

Back of the mountain: On the other side.

Jay hole: Space on a mountain road just wide enough for two teams or two vehicles to meet and pass.

Slipe: A tract, or slice, as in a poorly defined piece of farm land—"You better put the bush hog [big lawn mower] to that slipe crost the river.

Makes into: Becomes; foot and cart paths make into reg'lar roads.

Go through the country: Travel by automobile rather than by plane, train, or bus.

Room enough to cuss a cat without getting fur in your teeth: Elbow room; opposite of not enough room to change your mind.

Not nary a single one; not a single solitary one: Absolute zero.

Not a stitch: Nothing.

Nary a scale: Caught not a fish; got skunked.

Precious few: Damned few.

Several: A good many; a right smart; more than a few.

Whole heap; a heap of; a sight of: A lot of; a lavish of; a lavish plenty.

Lavish: A whole heap; a lavish of buggy whips became surplus when Henry Ford put his show on the road.

Lashin's an' lavin's: An abundance; plenty and some to spare; more than you can shake a stick at in a whole week.

Slathers: Plenty.

More than Carter's got pills: Much; many. Refers to Carter's

Little Liver Pills; predates "More than Carter's got peanuts."

More than a plenty: A gracious plenty; more than enough for now.

Slue: A raft of; a sight of; more than a show dog can jump over.

Chance: Quantity, as "We got a right good chance of cow peas."

As tall as a steeple: The tallest landmark on the horizon, used to be.

Clear: Clean; all the way, as "From Rock City you can see clear to no tellin' how far."

Clean up to the ellen yards: Said of a female whose dress is so short she shows all she's got—you can see her Christmas.

Along about: Approximately, as "We went ashore along 'bout ten."

As high as a cat's back: 'Way up.

As high as: As much as; an amount, as in "I'd go as high as three bucks for a Moon Pie rat now," and, "We raised as high as a bale a acre."

In a coon's age: Longer than a sleepless night; a long time; long enough to learn to survive in the woods; it takes a good coon dog to tree a coon, a better one to whip one.

In the room of: In place of.

From here to Haw River: All the way, as from hell to Jericho, or from hell to breakfast, or from Burwell's Bay to Antioch; from limit to limit.

All over hell and half of Georgia: A considerable area, especially if you're a-lookin' for somebody.

Country mile: Most any long distance.

# Of Time and Space and Place

A fur piece: The ultimate in distance and not easily reached.

Down the road a piece: Perhaps a country mile, depending on whether you ride or walk; you know it's a fur piece if you wear out your brogans from the inside.

A right smart piece: A long way but within reach between meals.

Close catch: Within easy reach.

A little piece: About as far as you can chase a child without losing patience.

In hollerin' distance: Less than two hoots an' a holler.

Two hoots an' a holler: Two curves and a cuss fight.

Sight: The distance that can be seen from a road.

Two sights and a look; two good looks and a dog bark: Two sightings and a long walk.

Howdy and a half: About a tater chunk—as far as you can throw a potato.

A hop, skip, an' a so-so: Same as above.

No piece a-tall: About as long as flavor lasts in chewing gum.

Coonskin with the tail thrown in: A loose and informal method of estimating length.

Rooster step: An indefinite span of time and distance.

Smidgen: A tad more than a mite.

Skimption: A small amount; hardly enough to bother with.

Swunk up: Shrunk up; shriveled.

Up: Caught up with; even with, as when you've caught up with plowing or with getting your ashes hauled.

Set: Deposit, as when one is ferried across the Cashie River and set on the other side.

Ferninst: Against; leaning next to; opposite to; across from.

The side next to the fence: The right side; the off side of a horse.

Run into: Expend or exceed beyond expectations; projects such as courtship and automobile repairs have a way of running into more time and money than was anticipated.

Settled age: When you're old enough to know better.

Stay place: A temporary or overnight shelter, as for hikers on the Appalachian Trail.

Fattenin' day: The first Saturday after payday.

Settlin' day; settlement day: October the first, when all accounts in a tenant-farm operation should be satisfied.

Limit day: March the first, when cotton plantation tenants and sharecroppers drew the first advances for rations—furnishings—with the start of the new year of farming.

Draw day: The weekly date to draw rations from the plantation commissary or the company store.

Chinch haulin' day: Moving day.

Vine day: May 16, the day for planting such as cymlin's, watermelons, mushmelons, cucumbers, gourds.

Turnip day: July 26. "The twenty-sixth of July, wet or dry, always sow turnips," former President Harry S Truman said. "Along in September they'll be four, five, maybe six inches in diameter, and they're good to eat—raw. I don't like them cooked."

Heartbreak day: New Year's Day; to slaves in the Old South a day signifying the trials and horrors peculiar to "the peculiar institution" and the separation of families.

Sales Monday; swap day; trade day; boneyard day: The first Monday in the month and time for trading livestock in sales usually near the county courthouse.

High time: Quite time; it's about time.

Dinner-gettin' time: Time to collect the ingredients for the up-coming noon meal.

Feedin' time: Time to feed up; time to feed the stock.

Quittin' time: Time to hang up the apron, punch the clock, take out the mules.

Out like Lottie's left eye: Out—and absolutely out. The phrase relates to Lottie Deno, native of Kentucky and a card dealer in New Mexico and Texas during the Great Buffalo Extermination of the 1880s. Her associates included Big Nose Kate Fisher and Doc Holliday.

     Germane and offered in the interest of old times is an old nursery rhyme:

> William A. Trimbletoe
> He's a good fisherman;
> Ketches his fishes,
> Puts 'em in dishes;
> Ketches his hens,
> Puts 'em in pens.
> Some lay eggs,
> Some lay none.
> Wire, briar, limberlock,
> Set and sing till 10 o'clock.
> Hickory, dickory, dock.
> Mouse runs up the clock;
> Clock falls down;
> Mouse runs roun';
> O-U-T spells out.

# Some Strong Words and Loose Talk

*Secretary of State Cordell Hull, a native of Tennessee, was an accomplished, dignified, and incisive cusser. A lisp lent a lilt to his lacings.*

*President Franklin D. Roosevelt liked to mimic Mr. Hull's most frequent expletive, "Jethuth Chwith."*

*Another of the Secretary's frequent comments was "pith ant."*

*Jonathan Daniels, once of President Roosevelt's White House staff, told us of two instances of Mr. Hull's expression of indignation:*

*—In remarking on Undersecretary of State Sumner Welles, Mr. Hull said: "Every department has its thun of a bitch but I've got the all-American."*

*—When Raymond Moley, at the Economic Conference in London in 1933, seemed to undercut him, Mr. Hull said: "That pith ant Moley. Here he curled up at mah feet and let me stroke his head like a huntin' dog and then he goes and bites me in the ath."*

# Some Strong Words and Loose Talk

*Secretary Hull's talent for cussin' got norated nationally with the Japanese attack on Pearl Harbor when, later that day, the Japanese emissaries, Ambassador Nomura and Special Envoy Kurusu, called at the State Department and submitted a prepared statement.*

*The Japanese were received coldly and formally, as President Roosevelt had instructed. But before the day was ended the word got out that Mr. Hull had chastised the visiting diplomats "in strong Tennessee mountain language."*

*We have often wondered what Mr. Hull said when he gave the envoys a piece of his mind—when he read their titles clear—on that memorable day.*

*The Secretary, in his memoirs, made a diplomatic disclaimer. He said he told the Japanese that in 50 years of public service he had "never seen a document that was more crowded with infamous falsehoods and distortions." He had heard that he cussed out the envoys, he wrote. "But the fact is that I told them exactly what I said above. No 'cussing out' could have made it stronger."*

*There Mr. Hull rested his case. The better story to the contrary stayed alive, however, and speculation continued, for good stories die hard. Years after the incident, Jonathan Daniels wrote us that Harry Hopkins, President Roosevelt's close and trusted confidant, "is authority for the fact or legend" that Mr. Hull did indeed use strong Tennessee speech that day to express his indignation.*

*Most of Mr. Hull's purple passages of that day may be lost to history. But a single fragment remains.*

*In about as diplomatic a cussin' as he could lay on, Mr. Hull, in pure East Tennessee dialect, addressed the envoys as:*

*"You hick'ry headed pith anths."*

---

Any amount but Rocky.Mount: Blatant bluffing on how much you'd bet before seeing the last card.

Jawin' an' joreein': Exchanging harsh words such as "You make my ass want to chew tobacco" and "You make my ass want to bite corn cobs."

I nevah run into any man what could out me: I can't be surpassed, exceeded, whipped, outdone.

Blowin' off, loudin' off, mouthin' off: Talking big; runnin' off at the mouth.

I'll cloud up an' rain all over you: I'll inundate you with bodily harm.

I'm a good mind to tie your asshole in a knot: I've been layin' off to frail (whip) hell out of you.

I'll tan yore hide till it won't hold shucks: I'll cut the blood out of you.

Pull in your horns: Quieten down; don't intrude; let somebody else have a say-so.

Hold your tater, hold your water: Same as above.

I'll cut yo' ass too thick to fish with an' too thin to fry: Sort of like what Bill (Bojangles) Robinson, native of Virginia, once announced at Harlem's Wishing Tree—he said that if he ever met up with Adolph Hitler he would cut him three ways: high, wide, and deep.

I read his titles clear: Gave him what for; gave him down the country (hell).

He preached his funeral: Same as above.

Flatted him: I flat out told him off in derogatory terms; gave him his walking papers.

Keep my name out of your mouth: I don't want to hear another word out of you either.

Rest your features: Shut up; hush up.

I'll tell you how the cow ate the cabbage—stalk and all: Euphemism for President Carter's threat to whip Senator Kennedy's ass.

I'll show you where the bear sat in the buckwheat: I'll show you who's boss.

Sit down before you fall down: Shut up and sit down before you get knocked down.

I'll cut your water off and take the meter out: I'll take you down a peg or two; I'll take you down a few notches; you'll get what's comin' to you.

I'll spring your staves: I'll bust your ribs.

Hessian; hayshant: An epithet usually reserved for a disobedient or defiant child; a throw-back to the Revolutionary War in America when hired Hessians fought for the Crown. My mother used to say, with some frequency, "I'll slap you windin', you little Hessian you."

Army worms: Opprobrium for Southern speculators in commodities during the Civil War.

Yore mammy trotted to Winston-Salem under an apple wagon: You are a son of a bitch.

He had one mother and a lot of fathers: Same as above.

I knew you when you won't—an' you still ain't.

I'm so hongry I could eat a bull an' it bellerin'.

I thought you went to shit and the hogs et you.

If you want to get froggy, go ahead and jump: Spit across my line, I double dare you.

Cross my heart and hope to die and go to hell the next minute: Either a preface or a conclusion to an absolute, unvarnished, brutal, and plain flat-out truth—or maybe a barefaced lie.

# With Your Feet
# Under the Table

*How do you like them ersters?*

> —Mayor Robert S. Maestri's only
> comment, as host to President
> Franklin D. Roosevelt at a
> luncheon in New Orleans;
> Mayor Maestri was said to
> have had "an aversion to
> extended speech."

*I recalled the case of a man and his wife who made a gas-tronomical tour of the nation for a magazine some years ago.
They roamed through every section of the country, sampling
the regional cuisine and reporting on it. One evening they were
in a South Carolina city, dining at a restaurant that had been
strongly recommended.*

    *"What is the soup du jour?" the wife asked the waiter.*
    *"Cowpea soup, ma'am," the waiter responded.*

*The lady's eyes widened. She looked at her husband, but he was studying the menu.*

*"Well," she announced weakly, "I said I'd try anything, and I guess if you're willing to serve it, I'm willing to try it."*

*This lady had character, courage, poise, and a strong stomach, otherwise she could have provoked a nasty incident in that restaurant. As it was, she enjoyed her cowpea soup with the realization that she had been a victim of regional differences in speech.*

—H. Allen Smith in
The Rebel Yell

Spread the table: Set the dining table.

Lay: Set, as "Lay an extry plate at the chirrun's table."

Grace the table, wait on the table, bless the table: Ask the blessing. "Son," a visiting preacher admonished, "keep yore eyes on them chess pies whilst I say grace."

Graces vary. Rare is this one: "Bless this meat; damn the skin; put back yore ears an' cram it in." And this when an unexpected guest caused a change in menu: "Lord, we thank Thee the dinner's been mended; chicken an' dumplin's when collards were intended."

Talk to the table, 'turn thanks to the table: Same as above.

Take an' rake, rake an' scrape: Help yourself to what's on the table.

Fall in for vittles, go ahead, take out: Set up an' fall in.

Let's get greasy aroun' the mouth: Same as above.

Settle the coffee and let's eat: Ditto. Boiled coffee is settled—

the grounds sent to the bottom of the pot—by adding a slosh of cold water or by adding eggshells.

Put the feed bag on: Ditto.

Fix your own plate: Serve yourself.

Cram it in with both fingers and stomp it down with both feet: Eat hurriedly.

Fingers were made before forks: An excuse for bad manners.

Plate of soup visit: Eat and run.

Stew the dishrag: Lay on a lavish repast; cook up a storm; put the big pot in the little one and fry the skillet.

Not too much of a tablecloth showed: Households where they set a good table. Surveying the scene in her home, my great-grandmother, Sarah Jeanette Boone Wilder, often added to the grace, "Help yourself at both ends."

Tight enough to crack a tick on: A grandchild's belly after a meal at grandma's.

Plan'ation fare: Chicken every Sunday.

After-effects: Dessert.

Sonker, apple slump: A deep-dish fruit pie sweetened with molasses. The name comes from the advice, on being handed a ladle or dipper: "Sonker down to the bottom of the pan."

More than a plenty: A gracious plenty; more than enough for now.

Seven-course meal: A six-pack of beer and a possum.

Enjoyin' hoghead: Vittling.

Piecin': Nibbling, as "I got me a poke of groun' peas an' I been of a-piecin' all day."

Sawmill lunch: A can of sardines or a can of Vienna sausage, a handfull of soda crackers, and a bottle of soda pop.

Moonshiner's lunch: Same as above.

Co-cola, dope: A carbonated beverage.

Chitlin strut: A party where you drink likker, eat chitlins with cornbread, collards, sweet taters—no sweat, no strain, no pain.

That'll eat: That will make good vittling.

Georgia ice cream: Grits. A Yankee by name of Ulysses S. Grant, who once came South on business, liked grits soufflé.

Cincinnati ham: Salt pork; streaker-lean, streaker-fat, pork side meat with one or more streaks of lean within the fat. You're missing plenty if you haven't had fried side meat with navy beans or molasses; side meat is essential in the cooking of greens.

Arkansas chicken: Same as above.

Texas chicken: Ditto.

Middlin', middlin' meat: Pork, between shoulder and haunch.

Mud flop sandwich: A boiled pig's ear with barbecue sauce, served between slices of lightbread.

Cold collards sandwich: Cold collards between slabs of cornbread or a halved cat head biscuit.

Roas'n' ears: Ears of corn, well filled-out and fresh from the patch; for proper presentation they are roasted or boiled and buttered.

Lye hominy, big hominy: A food product; a staple; a device to make use of corn after the growing season in some form other than corn meal, frozen corn, or corn whiskey. Lye hominy is shelled corn from which the hulls have been removed by soaking in lye made from ashes, preferably of oak and hickory. One gallon of shelled corn makes two of hominy. A self-respecting moonshiner will make a gallon and a half of corn whiskey from a bushel of corn, but a greedy one will double production by using sugar in the fermentation process.

Hominy, pone, and samp, an old word for grits, are from the language of Indians of the South.

Cush: Eggs, water, leftover cornbread, and diced onions, mixed with bacon grease, stirred in a frying pan, and cooked to the consistency of oatmeal. Dr. M. M. Mathews, in *Some Sources of Southernisms*, says that cush is an Arabic word brought from Nigeria and Angola by slaves.

Sugarhouse molasses: Table syrup.

Long sweetenin': Molasses.

Short sweetenin': Sugar.

Gunjers: Ginger or molasses cookies. The word gunjers is Arabic in origin.

Poor do: Dumplin's of bread scraps dampened with water and baked; a concoction made by stirring corn meal and grease in a skillet, frying until it smokes, then adding water or milk.

Cornbread an' common doin's: Cornbread and pork.

Hog an' hominy: Plain fare; common doin's.

Wheatbread and chicken fixin's: Lightbread and chicken fricassee. Dickens, in his 1842 visit thiswards, preferred lightbread and chicken fixin's because, in addition to chicken, the blue-plate special of the time included "broiled ham, sausages, veal cutlets, steaks, and other such viands of that nature as may be supposed, by a tolerably poetical construction, to 'fix' a chicken comfortably in the digestive organs of any lady or gentleman."

Boil the pot: Cook a vegetable dinner.

Yam: The succulent red-meated sweet tater, not to be confused with the white. Yam is a Guinea word introduced into Virginia prior to 1676.

Look: Examine; before cooking greens or beans, they should be washed and looked thoroughly to remove bugs, pebbles, trash.

Blubber up: Bubble.

Basket dinners: Vittles packed in oak split baskets for serving at all-day church functions with dinner on the grounds.

Put out: Basket dinners are put out, or removed from baskets, and displayed on picnic tables for easy examination and selection of goodies.

Put up: Preserve, by canning mainly, fruits and vegetables.

Stir: A quantity of apple butter; three bushels of apples will make a stir.

Horse-head stirrer: A wooden implement used in the making of apple butter; the contraption resembles a child's play horse with a blade at a right angle to the handle.

Blue john: Skimmed milk.

Blinky: Slightly sour milk.

Turns: Milk for churning begins to turn sour—turns into clabber—when warmed beside an open fire or close to a wood-burning cook stove.

Switchell: Half a cup of honey, half a cup of cider vinegar; or a combination of molasses and water with vinegar, cider, or rum. For a refreshing drink on a hot day, add four teaspoons of switchell to a dipper of well or spring water.

Stick-to-the-ribs food: Country cookin', as collards, cornbread, beans, potatoes, pork.

Bought vittles: Convenience foods.

Fodder: Eat, as in "Jack Bleeck's used to be a good place to fodder."

Roll your lunch: Pack your lunch.

T'eat bucket: Lunch pail, a contraction of "to eat."

Board around: Shift around, as a teacher in a one-room old field school depended on one patron after another for bed and board.

Somethin' t'eat: Wants some rations rat now.

I'm so hungry my stomach thinks my throat's been slit: Hungry enough to put a hurtin' on—to consume most of—whatever is available.

Organ recital: Rumbling from an empty stomach.

Drown the miller: Too much of a good thing, as when one adds too much water to a drink of whiskey, or too much milk or water in making bread; the term also denotes that flour is low in the barrel.

Empt'ns: A watery mixture of dough left to ferment in a crock; a frontier form of sourdough starter.

Dustin' of salt: A tad.

Struck through: When salt has penetrated the flesh of an unscaled fish. When one intends to roast a mullet on a spit, you gut it but don't scale it, then salt it thoroughly. When the salt has struck through, rinse off the excess and put the fish to the fire.

Red-eye gravy, speckled gravy, calico gravy: A gravy made of grease from fried country ham—add a couple of sloshes of black coffee and boiling water and stir. Goes best with ham, eggs, and grits, and when poured over hot biscuit. Another good route: stir into molasses and sop with biscuit.

Slow gravy, bulldog gravy: Thick gravy, usually thickened with flour.

Life everlasting: Gravy made from country ham grease, milk or water, and flour.

Sawmill gravy: Same as above.

Poor man's gravy: Gravy made with most any grease and flour and water.

Texas butter: Gravy of steak grease, flour, and water.

Streak gravy: Gravy made from streaker-lean, streaker-fat bacon, or from home-cured bacon grease and water.

Biscuit block: A waist-high block of oak, smooth on top, for the making of beaten biscuit. The baker attacks the biscuit dough, mounted on the block, with a wooden instrument resembling a shortened baseball bat and beats like the devil beating tanbark until the dough breaks out in blisters.

Cut biscuit: Biscuit formed by using a device such as a biscuit cutter, an inverted tin can, water glass, or coffee cup.

Broke biscuit: Biscuit formed by squeezing or pinching.

Cat head biscuit: Large biscuit about the size of a cat's head.

Belly breakers: Same as above.

Scratch biscuit: Handmade from scratch; nothing from a refrigerated container.

Biscuit with a hole in it: A biscuit into which cane syrup or black strap (New Orleans) molasses is poured into a finger-punched hole on the side.

Grudjin's: Biscuit made of lard, cornmeal, and hop leaven.

Tater riffle: Lightbread; a loaf of yeast-raised wheat bread.

Fatty bread: Cracklin' bread, usually made with corn meal, sometimes with flour, and cracklin's, of course.

Johnny cake, journey cake: Cornmeal cake baked crusty and brown on an open fire; it is made by pouring a mixture of meal and water—no baking soda, salt, buttermilk, or shortening—over hot coals and covering with more coals. Indians in southern regions baked such cakes to sustain them on long journeys.

Corn dodger: A small cornmeal cake fried in a pan or baked on a stove lid.

Hoe cake: A cake of cornmeal baked on a hoe blade held or propped over an open fire.

Red-horse bread: Hush puppies. Hush puppies developed in the days when family dogs had the run of the house and at meal times got underfoot and rambunctious and created such bedlam that cooks threw them dollops of fried cornbread. With the beneficence went the admonition "Hush, puppy."

Today hush puppies are sorry confections of cornmeal, flour, and, of all things abominable—sugar.

Warning: Chances are that if you order cornbread in most any Southern restaurant you won't get cornbread at all, but sugared hush puppies instead.

Crumble up: A rustic pick-up of cornbread crumbled in a glass of sweet milk and eaten with a spoon. Similar and easier on the gums is baked sweet potato crumbled in milk.

Charlie Taylor: A makeshift butter of molasses and kitchen

grease. Who was Charlie Taylor who gave his name to this sop?

Eating short: On short rations; in a tight; up against it.

Short commons: Same as above.

Long come shorts: Ditto.

We drunk some water and sucked our thumbs: We had short rations.

Missed-meal colic: A case of hunger.

Set back food: Vittles that have been cooled, then put on the table; leftovers.

Shorts: leftovers.

Totin': The practice of taking home food and other items from the kitchens of employers to supplement poor wages; totin' is usually done on the sly.

Totin' the crooked arm: Heading home with purloined vittles in a vessel tucked close to the body.

Pots an' pans: Leftovers carried home by totin'.

Smack bones: Marrow bones; spare ribs of pork.

Mountain oysters: Lamb, calf, pig, and turkey fries; testicles. Any man who won't eat mountain oysters wears lace on his drawers. "Are these the kind of oysters you put on a rock and crack?" "No. These are the kind you put on a crack and rock."

Prairie oysters, Oklahoma oysters: Same as above.

Chicken slick: Chicken stew and pastry.

Chicken bog: A stew of chicken and rice, sometimes with sausage added.

Haslet: A hearty stew consisting mainly of the edible viscera of

the hog—heart, liver, lights—and made more savory by liberal application of red pepper, sage, and onions. An ancient and honorable wintertime dish, dating from the fourteenth century, now in disrepute and short supply because of alleged contamination found by microscopic examination in the lights, or lungs.

Freshies, freshlets: Specific pork parts including brains, liver, lights, heart, chitlins that can't be set back and stored; unlike hams, shoulders, and slabs of bacon, they must be consumed immediately after hog killin'.

Maryland end: Ham hock. The big portion of the ham is the Virginia end.

Muddle, mull: A stew, usually with fish or squirrel as the main ingredient; as in rockfish muddle or squirrel muddle.

Gumbo, gombo: A soup of New Orleans provenance. Okra is the basis and probably gave the concoction its name, for okra came from Africa and in the Angolan language is *kingombo*. Gombo, said Lafcadio Hearn, is the generic term for "various culinary preparations . . . compounded of many odds and ends, with the okra-plant, or true gombo, for a basis."

Mess, bait: A quantity of vittles, cooked or acquired for cooking; generally just enough for one—enough collards, or cow peas, or turnip sallet to smack your bill over.

Cackling fart: An egg.

Dressed eggs: Deviled eggs garnished with parsley.

Bright-eyed eggs: Sunny side up.

Saucered an' blowed: Coffee that's been cooled down; you've poured some from cup to saucer and funneled your breath across it. Also means everything is hunky-dory, on schedule, on the beam, A-OK.

Barefooted: Coffee without sugar or cream. "Laced with the ardent" is black coffee boosted with a shot of booze.

With socks on: Coffee with cream.

Egg coffee: Boiled coffee with egg shells in the pot to settle the grounds.

Coon-ass coffee: Chicory, mostly, boiled, black, and strong. Some coffee is so weak you can stand in a barrel of it and see your toes. Some is stout enough to talk back to the Big Sheriff.

Seed-tick coffee: An improvisation in the name of coffee. It was the week of "big court" in Roxboro, North Carolina, and the hotelkeeper ran out of coffee. He made do with what he could find—small, greenish beans that he parched, ground, and boiled. "Seed-tick coffee," he told his pleased patrons, neglecting to note that seed ticks are juvenile wood ticks that haven't yet tasted blood.

Pin the dish rag: Expel someone from the kitchen. Cooks may expel someone on whim or for serious infractions, ranging from being too much underfoot or telling the cook how to cook, to failing to keep the woodbox full or trying to put sugar in cornbread.

Cooked to a turn: Exactly right.

Won't quit: An always useful term to compliment the cooking, as in "These here vittles won't quit but I'll hafter."

It would put yore granny in the branch: The food is so good it would; another compliment.

No thank you, I've reached: I've et so much my stomach is touching the table—the top of the line in compliments.

# Side Gals, Randy Bucks, and Makin' Out

*In presenting this souvenir to my multitude of friends, it is my earnest desire to, in the first place, avoid any and all egotism, and secondly to impress them with the fact that the cause of my success must certainly be attributed to their hearty and generous support of my exertions in making their visits to my establishment a moment of pleasure. While deeming it unnecessary to give the history of my boarders from their birth, which would no doubt prove reading of the highest grade, I trust that what I have written will not be misconstrued, and will be read in the same light as it was written; and in mentioning that all are born and bred Louisiana girls, I trust that my exertions in that direction will be appreciated as yours has been to me.*

> —From a promotion piece for
> Lulu White's famed New
> Orleans bordello, "Mahogany
> Hall"

*If it weren't for the married men we couldn't have carried on at all. And if it weren't for the cheating married women we would have earned another million.*

>—Minna and Ada Everleigh,
> natives of Kentucky and
> operators of "The Everleigh
> Club," a famous sporting
> house in Chicago.

Ask for her company: Try for a date with a Southern belle, such as Tallulah Bankhead, Ginger Rogers, Pearl Bailey, Mary Martin, Nancy Langhorne (Lady Astor), Ava Gardner, Scarlett O'Hara, Lena Horne, Dinah Shore, Elizabeth Ray.

Wait on, keep company with; set up to, talk to, call on: Date.

Knock at the door, walk out with: Same as above.

Carry straws, shine up to, cut after, run after: More of the same.

Make sheep eyes, make time with, take a shine for: Ditto.

Sparkin', they've got up a case: Said of an early stage of courtship, when gifts are offered and accepted.

She's talkin' to him: She's interested.

Took a heart burnin': Fell in love.

Posy ring: What a swain offers after a spell of courtin'; symbol of proposal and engagement.

Jularker, jusem-sweet: Sweetheart.

Jularkin': Courtin'.

Carry: Escort, as in "Can I carry you to the box party?"

Arms her: What a gentleman does when he offers his arm in escorting a lady.

Warming over old soup: Reviving an old love.

Slippin' out of the traces: Have a roving eye; straying from the conjugal bower.

Steppin' out, steppin' aroun', slippin' with: Same as above.

Mess around: "Don't mess aroun' with calico when you've got silk at home."

Pirootin': Messing around; from "pirouetting."

Fun: Mess around; tom-cat; "When you fun with more'n one woman," an old tom cat said, "you want to foller ever' one what comes along."

Layin' out with the dry cattle: Said of young bucks who carouse most of the night with amiable gal chillun. When cows are dry they don't come in from pasture at night, and some women who are inclined to shirk domestic responsibilities are likewise nonchalant.

Shake down: An enticing dance "where you slide back an' show your linen." "Shift" was Shakespeare's word for "linen," a piece of a female's intimate attire.

Jazz, jass: American music in syncopated dance rhythms characterized by melodious themes. The word and the music got together in New Orleans in the late 1800s during Reconstruction, when New Orleans blacks began to acquire store-bought, not improvised, musical instruments. Their music progressed and with it the language and the word *jazz*—originally *jass*, a word shady in origin and sexual in connotation, meaning "speed up" . . . "excite" . . . "pep it up."

Jazz began spreading through the land during the First World War, and Rudi Blesh, jazz historian, gives credit for this to Josephus Daniels, then Secretary of the Navy. With his General Order No. 99, Daniels cut off the navy's whiskey rations and set the pace for more restrictions from Washington. Subsequently, on demands of both the navy and the army, Storyville, the famed New Orleans resort district, was closed. With the sporting houses shut down, musicians and whore ladies who had entertained in them had to look elsewhere for gainful employment. Thus, Kansas City, St. Louis, Chicago, and New York got rewarded with "Elgin Movements in My Hips, with Twenty Years' Guarantee." The whole wad.

Cod buster: An exercise in terpsichore when cheek-to-cheek slow dancing was a contact sport.

Side gal: One courted on the sly, or side, unbeknownst to one's steady.

Rang him the go-by: She refused his suit.

Got the mitten: Was flatted, kicked, jilted.

Hug-me-tight: A buggy with a seat hardly big enough for two.

Trollin': Gal chillun walkin' a beach in bikinis, wigglin' the bait.

Bank walker: A male with much to show in the way of an appendage. The term comes from skinny dippers in farm ponds and streams; those with small tools get in and out of the water in a hurry, while the heavy-hung parade their devices.

In the rise of her bloom: Reaching womanhood.

Twitchy britches: Hot to trot.

She's got her trottin' harness on: She's ready to go and ready for most anything.

Sap-risin' time: A time for loving.

Bad after: Horny.

Wild as a peach-orchard boar: A randy buck; sexually passionate and unrestrained.

> Lost is the derivation of the term, known at least from
> Virginia to the Ozarks. Perhaps it comes from a boar's belly
> ache after loading up on green peaches—seed and all. Or
> from the natural mating manner of a boar roaming in a
> peach orchard. Whatever . . .

> General Dan E. Sickles of the Union Army became
> known in the Civil War as "the hero of the peach orchard."
> He was known, too, as a randy buck. Any connection with
> "wild as a peach orchard boar" may be coincidental. Sick-
> les won his hero's laurels at Gettysburg when, holding the
> III Corps salient in Sherfy's peach orchard, his troops stood
> up to Longstreet's heavy artillery fire and infantry assaults
> before being driven out of the orchard and the adjacent
> wheat field on the second day of battle. Sickles won laurels
> of another sort for service in assorted boudoirs; age did not
> limit his interest in women, for when he attended a Gettys-
> burg reunion in 1913, he was accompanied by a young lady
> identified as an "attendant."

Peach-orchard crazy: Passionate; lascivious.

Ravin' for pleasure: A randy buck.

Hot as a billy goat in a pepper patch: She's a-pantin'; she's a
pushover.

Put; put out: If she's a pushover she'll surely put.

Come across: She would, and she did.

Piss elegant: Piss proud; piss hard; a false erection; after mic-
turition one often loses his eager or his muscle tone.

Blue-steel throbber: A penis poised for takeoff.

Jism; gism: Dog water; crotch oil; a by-product of foreplay; to "put a little jism to it" means apply extra effort.

Makin' out: Scoring in dalliance; socializing in boudoirs and in back seats of automobiles.

Oversported: Worn out from makin' out.

Jine off: Coupling with intent to make out.

They're doin' their weavin' at the same loom: They're makin' out.

Proud: In heat.

In season: Same as above.

She's a-bullin': Male call.

She pleasured him: Male called.

Rough-locked: Mated.

He saw her above the fish dam: He scored; she let him have some.

Ground rations: Sexual intercourse on a leafy bower in a bosky dell retreat.

In the short rows: The moments just preceding orgasm.

Jape: Shag; roger; monkey; tread; copulate. Passed along by Ernie Deane: "Little dogs do it an' stick to it, and birds do it on the fly."

Get liver for your pup, get gravel for your goose: Satisfy sexual appetite.

Lay some pipe, salt your beans, salt your meat: Same as above.

Get your ashes hauled, shake the grate: Same as above.

Catch up on your haulin': Ditto.

Plow at the forks of the creek, plow some weeds under: More of the same.

Poontang: A piece of pussy; a piece of snatch; a roll in the hay. Some word-watchers claim the word "poontang" was contrived by Edward Angley, native of Palestine, Texas, and a reporter on the old New York *Herald Tribune,* but this is not so. The term comes from *putain,* Louisiana French for "prostitute," and has been in use in the South since about 1870.

Hung by a serpent: Got with child.

Gaining weight: Pregnant; in a family way; blowed up.

Her apron is riding high: Same as above.

She wears the bustle wrong: Ditto.

Lusty: Ditto.

They planted corn a-fore the fence was built: They had a baby in progress before they married.

They done made their crop an' now they're a-buildin' a fence aroun' it: Same as above.

The baby didn't come early—the wedding came late: Ditto.

They ate supper before they said grace: Ditto.

She broke her leg above the knee: Got pregnant without benefit of clergy.

Sprained her ankle: Same as above.

Born on the wrong side of the blanket: Born out of wedlock.

Sunday baby: Base-born; base-begotten; off-child.

Come-by-chance child: Illegitimate; woods colt; bush colt; catch colt; old field colt; outsider; volunteer; yard child; bantlin'.

Ditch-edge chillun, straw-field chillun, sawmill child, buzzard baby: Same as above.

"Long-o'-de-pa" chillun: Those conceived "alongside of the path."

Briar-patch chillun: With pappies no more known than which briar scratched the rabbit. "Motherhood is a matter of fact, fatherhood is a matter of opinion"—an old quote.

Come-after child: One born after departure of the father, as in a broken marriage, or one whose father was killed at Gettysburg.

Fooled her: Promised to marry but didn't.

Fell a-foul of: The predicament of unwed Southern mothers who were served by predaceous Yankee soldiers.

Stand pappy: Assume paternity, as "I'll stan' pappy for yore baby."

On the carpet; on the floor: A couple being married.

Step off the carpet: Get married.

Jump the broomstick; jump the twig; jump the stick: Common law or simulated marriage ceremony; nuptials without benefit of clergy or justice of the peace.

Pairing: Living together with marriage intended whenever a parson or a magistrate comes handy; living in unsanctified relationship.

Knew: Was intimate with, as "He knew her before they married."

You didn't pick up a crooked stick: You didn't err in selecting a mate.

Been called to the straw: Pregnant and in her lying-in period;

in medieval England, "lady in the straw" meant giving birth in a primitive bed of coiled straw rope.

Pull fodder: Give birth.

Fly in the milk: Said of offspring of white and black parents.

Milk and molasses: Same as above.

He strowed his mess early: He got a soon start on sowing wild oats; he was quick to become a father.

She named it to him, she laid it on him: She said he was the father.

It was caught in his oven, it was caught in his trap: The baby may not be his'n but it's his wife's.

She put his leg in a sling: She cuckolded him.

She put horns on him: Same as above.

She's got more than one mule in her stable: She's an unfaithful wife, mistress, girlfriend.

She has many strings to her bow: Same as above.

Comb's red: In a state of sexual excitement; wants to marry.

Comb's turning red: Courtin' a-ready an' didn't wear black for a year after he died; she couldn't wait till he got cold.

# On Minding Your Manners If Raised Up Right

*This likker is just right.*
*If it had been any worse I couldn't drink it.*
*If it had been any better you wouldn't have give it to me.*
*—An old saying*

*Thar's the bed, an' hyere's the lanton. If you uns need anything else, jist tell us what hit is. An' then we'll tell ye how to do without hit.*

*—A North Carolina mountaineer*
*to an overnight guest*

How'd you find your mother?: The question has nothing to do with lost-and-found or discovering another's whereabouts. It pertains to one's well being—is your mother hale and hearty in mind and body?

Did you winter well?: A question in springtime of one not seen a-fore Christmas or a month of Sundays. A detailed answer is permissible.

How's ev'ybody?, how's ev'ything?, how y'all?: A friendly howdy-do to one or more people with no detailed response required or expected. The greeting is often made without breaking stride and the response, if any, is ignored.

Take care: Be heedful of most anything and nothing in particular. It means the same as "have a nice day" and is more palatable.

Will you take on wood?: Will you join me in a drink? This from riverboating when paddlewheel steamers tied up at landings to take on wood for fuel.

Let's wood up: Same as above.

Let's strike a blow for liberty: An invitation by Vice President John Nance Garner of Texas for one to join him in hoisting bourbon and water.

Let's cut the dust: Let's have a drink.

Let's take the oath: Bottoms up. After running the Federal blockade at Fort Fisher, North Carolina, during the Civil War, skippers and pilots customarily went below and "took the oath"—reaffirming high regard for each other's expertise and courage under fire.

Will you take the books?: A question handed along with the Bible and hymn book to the preacher or other person of piety visiting the home, inviting him or her to lead in family prayers.

## On Minding Your Manners

Will you make a beginning?: An invitation to one to say grace.

Stay an' see how the pore folks live: Eat with us—and be guest at a feast.

I don't care if I do: Although it sounds at first glance like a refusal, it is an acceptance.

Mighty mannerly, mighty mannerable: Well spoken; on good behavior; said of one who wears well.

Make your manners: Curtsy; remove your hat and hide your quid.

Looked on: Regarded, as in "Glen Rounds is looked on right well in some parts."

Got no rocks to throw at anybody: Everything is made for love.

Swap howdies: Exchange greetings.

Howdied but ain't shook: Acquainted but never introduced.

Too new a broom: Not well acquainted with.

Pass and repass: Speak when they meet but not on good terms.

Pass the time of day: Exchange small talk for a couple of minutes.

Let me speak at you: I want a word with you.

Strike up with, get up with: Come upon, meet, assemble with, as in "It's always good to strike up with such as Bennett DeLoach, Cal Goodrich, Jean Rousseau."

Run on, come on, run into: Meet unexpectedly.

Git down 'n' show yore saddle: Light 'n' hitch; light 'n' look at yore saddle; light down 'n' take grub.

Lift yore hat 'n' rest yore wraps: Come in an' warm; set a spell; set down an' cool off; rest yore features.

Put yourself level in a chair; y'all have chairs: Please be seated.

Make yourself to home: Welcome, and take your ease.

The latch string is always out: You all are welcome, no matter if anybody's at home or not.

Raisin' up, bringing up: Manner of being reared, as in "In my raisin' up a body'd better pay 'tention to what the old folks said."

Comes on you: Visits; when one comes on you at home and at meal time, you invite him to take out, to light 'n' set, and to have a drink and stay for supper.

Y'all come to see us, heah: A way to end an exchange of small talk and possible involvement or commitment; euphemism for "Good-bye . . . I'll see you later," or for "Here's my bus."

Y'all needn't run off: Good-bye if you won't set an' stay longer.

Come to see us and stay till nearly supper time: Stay as long as you can—I'm just kidding.

Tarred by the same bresh: You are as guilty as another. The term originally meant marking sheep with color, usually with a tar brush, to identify flocks.

Kissin' kin: Close enough to claim kin; if kin but not kissin' kin because of acne or politics, you are from the same breed of cats or tarred by the same bresh.

Kinnery: Family reunion types.

Our grandpas swapped horses: We're kin but don't claim it.

My grandpa's dog crossed his grandpa's pasture: Same as above.

Generation: Family; kind; breed; a kinship group from oldest to youngest, as in "The whole generation claimed to be half-French," and "The Horners were a generation of like-minded people—all ringy as all get out."

Chiswell Dabney Langhorne, of Danville, Virginia, raised a generation of five attractive daughters. One was Lady Nancy Astor, first woman to sit in the British Parliament; another married the artist Charles Dana Gibson and became the prototype of the famous Gibson girl.

Own-born cousin: First cousin.

Asshole kinfolks: Kin, but no closer than fourth cousins.

Cousinhood: Close kinship of families locked in by inter-marriage.

Cow cousins: No kin but weaned on milk of the same cow—what's the relationship when weaned by the same wet nurse?

Cousin to: Often last part of the query, "Who were you . . . ?" The questioner knows your name perfectly well but wishes to identify you with kinship to particular people. If you are kin to somebody in the line of Robert E. Lee, for example, you would be regarded by the ladies of the United Daughters of the Confederacy as quality beyond reproach.

Quality: Quality folk; people with class and pedigree.

Scrumpt: Tidied, as in "If I'd a-knowed you was a-comin' I'd a-scrumpt up my hair."

Shake yourself into order: Make yourself presentable.

Much: Praise; make a to-do over, as you much up a bird dog for a good point or a smart retrieve.

Yankee dime: Payment by a kiss for a small favor.

Stoking: Sharing the spoils of a hunt.

Go snooks: Go Dutch; pay equal parts.

Turn: A favor; a turnabout.

Lick thumbs: Reach an agreement on a financial obligation; for instance, you give your doctor a jug of apple brandy or an old ham to satisfy your bill fair and square.

Pay out: Settle a debt with a farm owner if you are a tenant, or with a time-store merchant if you are a farm owner, when crops are sold.

Lagniappe: A gift, something extra, as a piece of bubble gum to a child or a dog biscuit to a puppy at a bank's drive-in window. "A nice, limber, expressive, handy word," Mark Twain said. A word "worth traveling to New Orleans to get."
  Lagniappe is a Louisiana word by way of Spain and not in wide use today. No longer in general use either is the old Southern custom of "throwing in" a little something extra with a significant purchase. Mister Jim Dalrymple, of Sanford, North Carolina, used to throw in a shirt and a tie with your purchase of a three-piece suit of clothes.

Dance in the hog trough: What an older sister is supposed to do if a younger sister marries first.

Waiters: Wedding attendants.

Shoot: A euphemism; genteel Southern ladies who wear hats and tote parasols and gloves to attend meetings of the DAR and Colonial Dames often use the term if they forget to load their flasks.

Grape company: Visitors who come calling mostly when your scuppernong vines are heavy with goodies. Other such company comes when strawberries, peaches, watermelons, and cantaloupes are in season.

Go by: Stop by, as "Let's go by my place and have a drink."

Go to grass, go to Guinea: Mannerable reprimands; my Aunt Berdie's way of telling one to go to hell when she had the grammies—when she was annoyed or vexed. As in "Aw-w-w-w, go to Guinea. I've heard enough out of you."

Plague take it: Another of Aunt Berdie's euphemisms, this one doubtless meaning "Oh, shit."

Push: One pushes stalled automobiles, grocery carts, little old ladies off sidewalks, and biddies in the creek.

Mash: One mashes buttons for elevators and television programs, and mashes automobile horns, boiled potatoes, black-eyed peas, and cockroaches. Babies are mashed when squeezed with affection.

     H. L. Mencken traced mash, in the sense of beating or striking, to the Gullah dialect of the South Carolina and Georgia coasts. Some word-workers think Gullah is an archaic form of English, acquired and modified by black slaves who had lost their native languages and developed a second tongue. Studies of Dr. Lorenzo D. Turner, a Negro linguist, show that Gullah is really West African in origin and probably through fraternization of black and white children many Gullah words slid into Southern speech.

     Mash, in another definition, means the fermenting mess that moonshiners distill into whiskey that can leave one speechless.

Fitten: Right and proper; meet. Don Whitehead, twice a winner of a Pulitzer Prize for reporting and coauthor with his wife of an unpublished book on how to cook with bourbon, said of mint juleps: "Tain't fitten that a man should put grass in his likker."

## Like Grandpa and the Electric Fence

*Like a hotbed of tranquillity*

        *—Edward Durrell Stone's*
        *description of his birthplace,*
        *Fayetteville, Arkansas*

Like Claude Harris' mule: Indifferent. "Naw suh, he ain' blind," Claude Harris said as his mule plowed into a fence paling. "He jus' don' give a damn."

Like a jackass eatin' briars: Grinnin' like a barrel of possum heads.

Like a tall dog: In like Flynn; in like a burglar.

108

# Like Grandpa and the Electric Fence

Like a dog with two tails: Proud.

Like a rat-tailed hoss tied short in fly time: Exasperated.

Like a suck-egg dog: Shame-faced.

Like a chicken with his head cut off: Helter skelter; ever' which a-way.

Like a polecat at a camp meeting: Unwelcome.

Like a tall cow pissin' on a city sidewalk: Splattering.

Like a rooster in an empty henhouse: Angry.

Like the past of pea time: The garden has gone to pot.

Like something the cat drug in and the dog wouldn't eat: Like something chewed up and spit out.

Like a martin to his gourd: With sure instinct.

Like they do in Alabama: They do without.

Like a June bride in a feather bed: Hot as a two-dollar pistol; hot as a depot stove.

Like a bug arg'in with a chicken: Useless.

Like an old hen with one chick: Proud; fussy; busy.

Like a long-tailed cat in a room full of rocking chairs, like a porcupine in a balloon factory: Nervous.

Like a frog on a busy road with a busted jumper: Apprehensive.

Like bees in honeysuckle, like bees in a barrel of molasses, like bees on a watermelon rind: Buzzin' an' busy.

Like a turkey in young corn: Acres and acres, and all mine.

Like licking honey off a blackberry vine: It ain't easy.

Like getting an ox out of the ditch: Well nigh impossible.

Like what God gave a billy goat: A hard head and a clear conscience.

Like a cat in hell with no claws: Doomed.

Like the devil beating tanbark: Fast and furious; the most action since grandpa pissed on the electric fence. Tanbark is bark used in tanning after it has been beaten into bits and pieces.

Like the boy the calf ran over: Speechless.

Like a live oak limb: Crooked as a dog's hind leg.

Like a rubber-nosed woodpecker in the Petrified Forest: Confused.

Like a buzzard in a tree waiting for a mule to die: Patient.

Like a sow needs a sidesaddle: Unnecessary.

Like a cat with two tails: Unnecessary.

Like a duck after a June bug: Determined.

Like a popcorn fart in hell: Unnoticed; like a fart in a whirlwind.

Like a bear that's wintered in the balsams: Out of sorts. Balsams are mountain trees—fir, spruce—of the Southern Appalachians. Bears that have wintered, or hibernated, within them come out hungry and out of sorts.

Like a bear with a sore ass: Angry.

Like a jackass in a tin stable: Noisy.

Like salts in a widder woman; like salts in an eel: Fast as croton oil, a drastic cathartic.

Like a bat out of Georgia: Speeding.

Like a cross-eyed owl: Split decision.

# Like Grandpa and the Electric Fence

Like a tree full of owls: A confederacy of the smarts.

Like a hog loves slops: Couldn't be happier.

Like a mud fence daubed with chinquapins: Superlatively ugly. Chinquapins are the edible nuts of dwarf chestnuts.

Like a feller that's been shot at and missed: Luckiest man alive.

Like shuckin' a nubbin: Trivial.

Like a monkey on a bobwire fence: Cautious.

Like a horseshoe just out of a forge: Hot.

Like three feet up a bull's ass: Dark; rich.

Like tits on a boar hog: Useless.

Like a bear's ass in pokeberry time: Red.

Like a shedding rooster after a rainstorm: Woebegone; be-draggled.

Like a greased wagon running in sand: Quiet and soothing.

Like a lost dog in a meat market: In a frenzy.

Like a partridge in pea time: Plump.

Like a turd floating in a backwater eddy: Aimless.

Like last year's crow's nest with the bottom out: Useless.

Like forty miles of rough road: Rugged in face and disposition.

Like an Arkansas preacher can spot a counterfeit nickel: Pronto.

Like shearing a pig: Big squeal and little wool.

Like splitting gum logs in August: Sweaty labor.

Like somebody stole his clothes when he was in swimming: Angry.

Like taking onions without salt: A kiss without a moustache.

Like the hub of hell: Hot.

Like buzzards roosted in it: One's mouth after a night of corn whiskey.

Like trying to sneak daylight past a rooster: Stupid.

Like pitch to a wagon wheel: It hinders more than it helps.

Like a spring lizard in a henhouse: Lively.

Like a cotton gin in packin' time: Jimber-jawed; a nonstop talker; huffin' an' puffin'.

Like a four-horned billy goat: An aggressive show-off.

Like a calf in clover: Antic; playful.

Like a short dog in high grass: Lost.

Like a brood sow in mud: Indolent.

Like putting a wildcat in a croaker sack: An impossible dream.

Like he's been hit in the ass with a rotten apple: He's acting like he's drunk.

Like a peach orchard bull: Sitting pretty; getting his.

Like Blalock's bull: Out; sweating; ornery. That bull of Blalock's, whoever he was, was versatile.

Like a child that's lost his chewing gum on a henhouse floor: Makes you want to tune up and cry.

Like flies in August: Thick.

Like a dog in a slaughterhouse: Happy.

Like a widder woman's ax: Dull.

Like smelling whiskey through a jailhouse door: Enough to drive a toper up a wall.

Like a dog shittin' peach seeds: Shaking all over.

Like a tom cat needs a wedding license: Not a-tall.

Like a goose a-goin' barefooted: Eternally.

Like three truckloads of bean pickers without a foreman: Governor Marvin Griffin's description of a Georgia legislature.

Like a basket of chips: Pleasant and comforting. It's good to have a basket of dry wood chips to start a warming fire on a whole overcoat day.

Like a June bug with a cat after it: A gone goose. Vance Randolph said there is an Ozarks notion that geese begin life anew at each sunrise, remembering nothing of other days.

Like a dog killing snakes: With a violent shaking of the head.

Like a sow playing with rags a-fore a storm: Same as above.

Like a cat trying to eat a grindstone: Impossible.

Like a long-eared mule in a buggy harness: Incongruous.

Like a speckled puppy under a red wagon: A pretty sight.

Like a calf kicking yeller jackets: Restless as a cockroach in a hot skillet.

Like a rabbit in a lettuce patch: Feisty.

Like a country-store dog: He lounges about a pot-bellied stove, hunts with anybody, is loyal to nobody.

Like a country dog coming to town: He'll piss on every post. Said of a political figure who tries to be all things to all people, and who takes a firm stand on all sides of an issue.

Like the alligator: Make like one and drag your ass out of here.

Like a clam at high tide: Happy.

Like a woodpecker with a headache: Hungry.

Like piss ants out of a log when t'other end's a-far: They pour out.

Like a toady frog under the drip of a house: Happy.

Like pushing a wheelbarrow with rope handles: Like shooting pool with a well rope.

Like a coon in a hollow log: Comparatively safe.

Like a long-eared mule: Contrary.

Like stretching a gnat's ass over a washtub: Awful.

Like a stack of black cats: Dark.

Like the skunk said when the wind changed: I knew it would come back to me.

# Reflections on the Political Scene

*I never voted for but one Democrat in my whole life and by damn, that year the corn never got knee-high and turned yaller as a pumpkin.* —*A Kentuckian*

*I voted for a Republican once forty years ago and my coffee hasn't tasted the same since.* —*Another'n*

*Are you aware that Claude Pepper is known all over Washington as a shameless extrovert? Not only that, but this man is reliably reported to practice nepotism with his sister-in-law, and he has a sister who was once a thespian in wicked New York. Worst of all, it is an established fact that Mr. Pepper, before his marriage, practiced celibacy.*

—*George (Smooch) Smathers of Florida, in a 1950 campaign speech for the U.S. Senate; he won*

Coattail politician: One who depends on the favor of a more successful political figure.

Courthouse barnacle: One who sticks to the public tit.

Hogback: An independent voter; one who bolts from traditional party affiliation.

He'll get it: He'll win election; as in "He's a real antediluvian son of a bitch but he'll get it."

That's the ticket: Term of approval.

Who beat?: Who won the election?

Throw the hatchet: Exaggerate; tell lies; extend the truth.

Draw the long bow: Same as above.

Stretch the blanket: Ditto.

Bunk: Nonsense. Bunk comes from Buncombe County, North Carolina, and got into the language by way of Felix Walker, a member of Congress from that county, from 1817 to 1823. He delayed the vote on the Missouri Compromise and bored his colleagues with an empty speech. He refused to cut it short or get to the point and explained that he wasn't talking for benefit of his colleagues but for his constituents—he was talking for Buncombe.

Runnin' off at the mouth: Verbal diarrhea, an affliction common to political figures.

Outnigger: Exceed one's opponent in expressing anti-black hostility.

Cut and dried: Prearranged; no problem.

Has the wrong end of the poker: A loser.

Honey funk: To curry favor; to deceive by flattery.

Buying gingerbread, making peace: Buying votes.

Shell the brush; shell the woods: Campaign in depth; cover all bases.

Broke bad: Changed sides; shifted alliance. This is an especially reprehensible act when one jumps the traces and works and votes with the other crowd.

Cutter: A spoiler. Cutters don't run to win but to take votes from likely winners.

As far as you can throw a bull by the tail: You'd trust some political figures as far as a cat can spit.

Horse-high, bull-strong, pig-tight, and goose-proof: The fourteen-karat bamboozle. The term applied originally to fences and now pertains to political and financial schemes. The fourteen-karat bamboozle comment comes from Seminole Sam, a character in Walt Kelly's matchless Pogo cartoon strip (5-8-1956). Seminole Sam was based on Colonel Samuel Taylor Moore, newspaper man, magazine writer, Quiet Birdman (balloons), and good companion.

Yellow dog Democrat: A straight ticket man. He'll vote for a yellow dog if he's a Democrat.

Black Republican: Free Soilers. They wanted all newly admitted states kept free of slavery.

Jaybird Democrats: The winning faction in the Jaybird-Woodpecker War, 1888–90, in Fort Bend County, Texas. The Jaybirds represented the wealth and 90 percent of the white population and were traditional Democrats.

Woodpecker Republicans: The losing faction in the Jaybird-Woodpecker War. They consisted of about 40 officials and ex-officials of Fort Bend County government who claimed to be Democrats but held office and control for twenty years as a result of Reconstruction and blacks voting the Republican ticket. The Jaybirds ousted the Woodpeckers from their holes in the county courthouse after considerable blood-shed and hard feelings.

The names of the factions apparently originated with blacks. David Nation, husband of Carry A. Nation and the only white man in Richmond, the county's principal town, to call himself a Republican, often used the names in his newspaper dispatches to the *Houston Daily Post.*

A black who helped perpetuate the names was Bob Chappell, who worked for Henry (Red Hot) Frost, a Jaybird leader and keeper of the Brahma Bull and Red Hot Saloon. He often danced in the streets and sang of Jaybirds and Woodpeckers:

> The Jaybird flew
> To the Woodpecker's hole.
> The Woodpecker to Jaybird says,
> "Goddamn your soul."
> The Jaybird says,
> "You needn't fer to cuss,
> Fer I didn't come here to
> Stir up any fuss."
> The Woodpecker says,
> "I've my doubts."
> The Jaybird says,
> "I'll make you walk about."

> The Jaybird walks
> The Jaybird talks.
> The Jaybird eats with a knife and fork,
> The Woodpecker eats with a spoon.
> The Jaybird flew to the Woodpecker's hole,
> The Jaybird to the Woodpecker says,
> "I'll make you walk about."
> The Woodpecker says, "I've my doubts!"

Up Salt River: The day-after-election position of defeated candidates.

Johnson Pettigrew, in an 1849 comment on speech peculiarities in the Charleston, South Carolina, area, noted that after rice is planted in Low Country plantations, "It is desirable to overflow the land, but if the river be salt this cannot be done. . . . The dread felt by all of a salt river and the frequent remarks concerning the same, led me to suppose that the term, so rife in political talk, had its origin here, for no defeated candidate could possibly look more disconsolate than a rice planter up a salt river."

Now hear this for Kentucky as the point of origin: Kentucky's Salt River in the mid-nineteenth century was frequented by river pirates. Passage on the river was already dangerous because of its tortuous shallows and bars.

Sound on the goose: Politically orthodox; true to the cause of slavery. Please respond, gentle reader, if you know the derivation of "sound on the goose."

Fire-eaters: Southern duelists, circa 1828; later, Southern extremists and uncompromising Secessionists. Among them were William L. Yancey, Robert Barnwell Rhett, and Edmund Ruffin, credited with pulling the lanyard on the first artillery piece to fire on Fort Sumter.

Carpetbagger: A term of opprobrium applied to Yankee opportunists who settled in the South during and after the Civil War, some with all their possessions in carpetbags. The afterlight of history shows that many carpetbaggers were respectable citizens who came south for humanitarian and legitimate business reasons.

In earlier years the term applied to itinerant bankers who carried their negotiable assets in gritchels made of carpeting material.

Scalawags: Southern whites who, during the Reconstruction era, joined carpetbaggers and freedmen for profit and political power and formed the Republican party in the South.

Prior to the Civil War the word described scrawny cattle—a reflection on Scalloway, Scotland, a small island with scrubby horses and ponies—and lazy, shiftless people. It was easy to transfer the term to poor whites and antebellum Whigs who sided with Unionists against the traditional native leadership.

Taking umbrage some years ago at editorials in the *Charlotte* (North Carolina) *Observer,* which had lately been acquired by the out-of-state Knight chain, a South Carolina reader complained that the paper's editorials on racial problems were written by carpetbaggers. Not so, he was told. The writers were a South Carolinian and two North Carolinians.

"If there's anything that I hate worse than a carpetbagger," the reader replied, "it's a damned scalawag."

Snollygoster: A tadpole; a pretentious boaster; a political shyster. The *Dictionary of Americanisms* quotes "a Georgia editor" as defining snollygoster as "a pretentious boaster" and a "fellow who wants office, regardless of party, platform or principle, and who, whenever he wins, gets there by the sheer force of monumental talknophical assumnacy."

Whatever "talknophical assumnacy" is, deponent knoweth not. But we know the editor quoted was Colonel H. W. J. Ham. He was great shakes as a platform speaker, circa 1890, and on the northern lecture circuit was known as "the Cracker Chaucer."

The Colonel's son, Walter Ham, said his father applied the snollygoster tag to "a fellow who is continually side-wiping around after a little office which he can't get, and which he ain't got sense enough to fill even if he could get it."

President Harry S Truman, in his whistle-stop campaign in 1952, renewed interest in the term. This when he applied it to "a group of Republican obstructionists—men of little minds and mean aspirations—who have put party

above country and have worked for votes instead of peace."
"Republican snollygosters," he called them.

Snollygoster began life in the South as a collo-
quialism for tadpole, or polliwog.

Rat killin': A political outing. Time was, when corn cribs were
emptied in later summer and prepared for the storage of the
new harvest, rats were exposed and eradicated in neighborly manifestations of mayhem and good clean fun and
games. Rat killin's nowadays are gatherings of ardent and
fun-loving political partisans—political workers known
with affection as "trash-movers," "members of the rougher
element," "branchhead boys." They gather to renew faith in
party and faction and vow again to whup hell out of the
opposition. Booze and pork barbecue are never in short
supply, but windy speeching is.

Chicken bog: Formerly the main dish in wood-cuttin's in
southeast North Carolina and northeast South Carolina,
now an attraction in political gatherings in South Carolina's
Horry and Dillon counties.

Ms. Rita Jenrette, whose husband represented Horry
County in Congress and was tagged in the Abscam affair,
brought chicken bog to national attention when she said
she was fed up to here with Sandlapper political excursions
featuring chicken bog, alligator shoes, polyester suits, and
Moose Lodge ceremonies with members parading with
antlers on their heads.

Chicken bog is a mixture of chicken and rice, usually
cooked in an iron washpot out of doors, and served with a
heavy lacing of black pepper.

Shad plankin's: Political and social gatherings in Tidewater
Virginia and northeast North Carolina. Shad plankin's are
held in springtime when anadromous shad leave the ocean
and swim upstream through inland waters to mate and

spawn. The shad to be planked are dressed and nailed by their tails to oak planks, placed upright and slanting and adjacent to beds of hot coals. While they cook, slowly, the incipient diners usually drink confiscated evidence whiskey provided by the sheriff's office.

When eating is about to commence, someone with authority, maybe a United States Marshal, mounts a gum stump and commands: "All you sons uh bitches please bow yuh haids whilst somebody sez th' blessin'. You heah?"

Dough face: A contemptuous name for a pliable politician. The term was first applied by John Randolph of Roanoke to Northern congressmen who sided with views and demands of the South on the slavery issue. From 1844 to Lincoln's election, every president was either a Southerner or a dough face.

Dough faces also are masks, often handmade, worn by children on Halloween forays.

Maverick: An unorthodox or unbranded political or philosophical creature who pursues an independent and unbridled course with a loose party or group affiliation; an unbranded range animal of unknown ownership.

Samuel A. Maverick, native of South Carolina and a signer of the Texas Declaration of Independence, was the eponym for the term maverick. He was a lawyer and made no claim to be a cattleman. His name got into the language because of a bunch of cattle—four hundred head—he took in for a debt in 1847. He left them in the care of a shiftless slave who failed to brand the calves and let the herd wander. Maverick sold the herd, brand, and range nine years later to A. Toutant Beauregard. Whenever the new owner's cowboys found an unbranded calf, as they ranged over several counties, they called it a maverick and branded it.

Gobbledygook: Bureaucratic jargon. Maury Maverick of Texas,

and a member of the United States House of Representatives, explained in 1944 how he coined the word: "Perhaps I was thinking of the old bearded turkey gobbler back in Texas who was always gobbledy-gobbling and strutting with ludicrous pomposity. At the end of the gobble there was a sort of gook."

From John Ciardi, this definition of gobbledygook: "Linguistic utilizations intermediate to finalized specification and rhetorically structured to maximize optionalization of alternatives while preserving deniability interim-wise."

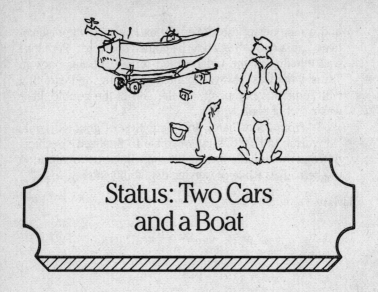

# Status: Two Cars and a Boat

*My old grandpappy didn't have no more l'arnin' than a pig's asshole. But he could spit further'n any man in Texas County.*
*—A citizen of the Missouri*
  *Ozarks bragging on his*
  *personal big dog in the meat*
  *house*

Big dog in the meat house: The number one guy. This was Ty Cobb's description of Sam Crawford, baseball's superstar when the Georgia Peach came on the big league scene.

Big buck at the lick: Same as above.

Tall hog at the trough, tush hog: Ditto. The tush hog—variation of tusk—has at least one and usually two enlarged teeth; it's fearsome to look at and to deal with.

Sittin' below the salt: Not in good social standing; low in the pecking order. The term came from old England: Once a day the feudal lord came to dinner in the great hall. From his dais he surveyed those seated at lower tables, the better folk nearest his table, the lesser farther away, below the salt cellar.

Nothing to write home about: No cause for bragging.

Live like a fighting cock: Indulge in high living with unlimited credit cards.

Above his raisin': Wants whiskey from a glass instead of a jug.

About to git above of herself: She served a six-course dinner, if you count the mints.

Raised on a floored pen: Brought up in ease and comfort. A hog raised on a floored pen and finished off with shelled corn produces lard and firm meat.

Prosperous as a prize hog at hog killin' time: One raised on a floored pen.

Rich as creasy: Rich as Croesus; rich as three feet up a bull's ass.

Rich as a Huguenot: With cash and social standing; finest kind. The phrase reflects on emigrant craftsmen who grew rich, rose in social position, and became leaders in South Carolina's Low Country aristocracy.

Stiff in the heels: Has plenty of money.

Eatin' long corn: In best financial shape ever.

They've got goose eggs an' new overhalls: They're in good standing with the bank.

Fixed: Financially secure.

Broke out with money: It shows all over.

Has money enough to burn a wet mule: Stinkin' rich.

High and palmy state: Not a care in the world; let the euphoria roll.

Shittin' in tall cotton, livin' in tall cotton: Prosperous; in good financial and/or social position; a good liver.

Got two cars and a boat: Has status, triple-distilled.

Eatin' high on the hog: Eating ham meat and doing good.

Living where the flitter tree grows close to the honey pond: Living in the land of milk and honey. Flitters are pancakes.

Over: More; a bonus, as in "I got as much as he got, an' over."

Bottom rail gittin' on top: Progress in community standing; the last shall be first.

Eatin' ham meat on sow-belly wages: Living above one's means.

In hog heaven and doesn't know it: He's gettin' his an' it don't cost him a single solitary cent.

Top down and pecker up: A dirt-road sport in an Austin-Healey.

Spankin'-bran'-new: Spitfire-new; bandbox-new.

He keeps his smokehouse greasy: He provides a good table.

Walkin' about in Zion: Got it made in the shade.

An empty sack: One too trifling to keep meat in the smoke-house.

Not a pot to piss in an' nary a window to throw it out of: You knew him when—before he got a brick house and a Burick arty-mobile.

Not a pot to piss in an' no bed to shove it under: Same as above.

Poor as gully dirt; dirt-dog poor: On the rim edge of poverty.

Clay eaters: Geophagists, people with calcium deficiencies who add hearth clay to a meager diet.

Will fare common: Won't be invited to sit at the head table.

The skimmin's of a drunken Saturday night: Trash.

They had to fry the nest egg when company came: They had a hard time holding buckle and tongue together.

They had a hard row to hoe: Were raised in mean circumstances.

Fried buckhorns and wahoo bark: A fanciful diet indicating extremely hard times.

They had to pump daylight in to make morning: They lived so deep in the woods they kept possums for yard dogs and a groundhog to tote the mail.

So poor he couldn't buy hay for a nightmare: So broke he couldn't even pay attention.

Up against it: In a tight; in a bind; in a squeeze for money.

Between a rock and a hard place: Broke as a busted trace chain.

Out of soap: Same as above.

Sugar is low in the barrel: When you are on your uppers and walkin' aroun' money is sca'ce.

Poor as Job's turkey: So thin he had to stand twice in one place to make a shadow.

We hasten to point out that the phrase "poor as Job's turkey" is not Southern in origin. Many students of the language assume it is Southern, and we include it so we can clear the confusion and set the record straight.

In the first place, in Biblical Job's day, turkeys were unknown in Asia Minor. Job never heard tell of one, and Biblical scholars can't find one in the Scripture. Likewise, Job's turkey isn't found in Southern folksay.

The phrase was coined and introduced into literature by Judge Thomas Chandler Haliburton, a Canadian writer of the nineteenth century whose work influenced such diverse authors as Henry Wadsworth Longfellow and Mark Twain.

One of Judge Haliburton's creations was Sam Slick, a Yankee storyteller who improved on the simile "as poor as Job" by adding a turkey—a turkey that was scrawny, enfeebled, and had only one tail feather, and was so weakly he leaned on the barn to gobble.

We thought you'd like to know. In the interest of good reporting, it is our pleasure to oblige.

It's a poor man's stay here: It's almost a hand-to-mouth existence.

Didn't have a tail feather left: Lost it all.

Small potatoes—an' few in the hill: Piddling.

# Farmin'—On the Old Plan'ation and in the Woods

When the winter goes, and when it gets to be time to burn off broom-sedge in the fields and underbrush in the thickets, I sort of want to cry, I reckon it is. The smell of that sedge-smoke this time of the year near about drives me crazy. Then pretty soon all the other farmers start plowing. That's what gets under my skin the worst. When the smell of that new earth turning over behind the plow strikes me, I get all weak and shaky. It's in my blood—burning broom-sedge and plowing in the ground this time of year.... Us Lesters sure like to stir the earth and make plants grow in it.... The land has got a powerful hold on me.

—*Jeeter Lester, in Erskine
Caldwell's* Tobacco Road

Bumblebee cotton: Cotton so stunted a bumblebee can squat on the ground and suck the blossoms.

Blowth of cotton: When cotton bolls burst and fields are white.

Cotton-field watermelon: A dwarf melon often found in cotton patches.

Lowgrounds: Bottom lands.

Wetted down and mudified: Lowgrounds after the river over-flowed.

Work public: When you quit farming and work for wages at any job excusin' farming.

At: The market price, as in "What's cotton at today?"

First Monday: A worn-out mule. The term refers to farm animals put up for public auction on the first Monday of the month.

Lay off: Establish boundaries of a garden plot, a tobacco field, a burying ground, and so on.

Task, tasking: The daily quota, the system of assigning daily quotas, for production by slave labor in South Carolina and Georgia Low Country rice, indigo, and cotton plantations. Under the task system a slave was assigned a certain amount of work for the day, after which he was free to do as he pleased. Under the gang system, in most plantation societies in the rest of the South, slaves were compelled to work from sunup to sundown.

 The basic task unit was a quarter of an acre, and today on St. Johns Island, South Carolina, a task is twenty-one rows in a quarter-acre unit. The task in plantation days was, for pounding rice, seven mortars—about two bushels all told—a day, and coopers were expected to make three rice barrels daily. The task for cotton pickers was ninety to one hundred pounds. Fence rail splitters were to split one hundred twelve-foot-long pine poles a day.

Turn: A quantity. A turn of stovewood is an armload; a turn, run, or jag of corn is all the shelled corn, usually two bushels, a man can tote in a sack to a grist mill.

Turn: Your place in line to get your grinding done; your putt.

Turns, evening turns: Chores before the day's work ends, such as doin' the milkin', feedin' up the stock, layin' in stovewood and firewood.

Run: A quantity of vegetables. Harvey J. Miller, author of *News From Pigeon Roost,* says in a note on Appalachian cookery that "a run of beans mean what you want to cook in a tub or vessel to put in stone crock or wooden tub for to make pickle beans."

Got his grinding done: He went to the grist mill, took his turn, and got his grain ground.

Make: Produce, as in "Our late peas didn't make this year."

Save: When a barn of tobacco is saved, it has been harvested and cured without having been destroyed by barn burning, hail, worms, or other pestilences that bug tobacco farmers.

Save: When a farmer or anyone else who fishes saves a limit of bass, he puts eight on his stringer.

Pull 'sang: Dig ginseng roots. Wild ginseng, regarded by Chinese as an aphrodisiac, is dug by 'sang hunters in the mountains of North Carolina, Tennessee, and Georgia. The work is chancy and hazardous. This from a buyer: "To harvest one pound, a man must walk not less than twenty miles over a two-day period, and in the process kill three rattlesnakes and ten copperheads."

Yarbing: Hunting for and digging ginseng and other herbs in mountain areas.

Bogged down: Land that's been cleared of brush. One also gets bogged down, or stuck, in sand dunes, income tax reports, and assorted jobs of work.

Get out: When it's too wet to plow and corn needs to be shucked, farmers often come indoors and get out, or shuck, ears of corn.

> Uncle Bud moved across the water
> To keep the boys from screwing his daughter.
> > Uncle Bud.
> Corn in the crib what ain't been shucked
> And a gal in the house what ain't been fucked.
> > Uncle Bud.
> > > —An old favorite

Feed up: Feed the livestock. Feedin' time comes after the day's work is done and before the farmer has supper.

Roughness: Fodder for the feeding of farm animals.

Foddering time: Time to pull, or strip, the almost dried leaves from standing corn stalks.

Maul rails: Split rails.

Snarly; gnarly: Said of twisted or otherwise damaged trees unfit for commerce.

Gentle the hogs; gentle the stock: Put out feed and salt for free-roaming animals.

Hog down: Turn hogs loose in corn and peanut fields to root what was left after harvesting.

Kill up: Archaic English for to butcher.

Work up: After killing hogs the meat must be worked up, or prepared for cooking and storage.

Old fields: Worn-out land. It is generally so poor it wouldn't sprout a cuss fight, or so poor two red-headed women couldn't raise a fuss on it.

It won't sprout a pea: Land so poor you have to sit on a bag of fertilizer to raise an umbrella.

Apple out: When vine crops such as cymlins, pumpkins, and maypops shed their blooms, they apple out. "Maypop" is a wild running vine along roadsides with bulbous fruit which bursts with a loud pop when stepped upon.

In the grass: A crop that needs weeding. Weeds often get a right good sling—a head start—if a farmer's hoe hands take sick or some other adversity develops.

Flag the crop: H'ist an old shirt on a pole in a farmer's field to remind him that he's behind in his weedin'. In North Carolina in the early 1860s work was regarded as the first duty of man and grassy cotton was well nigh sinful. Farmers who neglected to keep their fields clean were often subjected to ridicule—especially on Saturday nights at the train depot where loafers gathered. Here the crops of laggard farmers would be sold in mock auctions if they didn't promise to chop out the grass within the week.

Two-horse farm: About forty-five acres. Enough to keep two mules and a farm family busy.

House and found, house and furnish: Housing and provisions up to an agreed-upon limit, these to be provided by the farmer for his tenant or sharecropper.

Hoe hand; field hand; yard hand: Farm laborers.

Cattle ketch: A pen and ramp for loading cattle onto trucks.

Barnin': The harvesting of tobacco, as "We done barnin' yesdiddy."

Round up: The gathering together of domestic animals—cattle, sheep, hogs—after a year of fending for themselves in the wild. Predating cattle ranching, "round up" came into use in western North Carolina and Virginia and eastern Tennessee and Kentucky soon after those parts ceased to be frontier.

Hog claim: A share, by purchase, in the harvest of hogs that run wild and are to be claimed in a round up.

House: Harvest and store crops.

Pitch a crop: Plant a crop.

Raise a crop; make a crop: Grow and harvest a crop.

Raise some bread: Grow a crop of corn.

A fair yield: An understatement of production beyond expectations.

Push a plow: Follow a plow behind the south end of a northbound mule.

Take out: Unhitch an animal or team of animals from a conveyance or farm implement—a buggy, a wagon, a plow.

Strong: Fertile, as good soil is.

Buckshot land: Poor clay soil, so named for clay in small lumps.

Mulatto land: East Tennessee talk for dark soil with a clay foundation.

Crawfishy land: Porous soil.

Redbud land: Rich but rocky soil.

Beeswax mud: Yellow and sticky soil.

Stilards: Cotton scales, balance, steelyard.

Swamp: Clear of underbrush, as in "We swamped that ditch in no time a-tall."

Swamper: An old or spavined logger, so stove-up he can't work outside anymore and now swamps, or cleans, the bunkhouses.

Beezlin's, beastings: Beast milk; colostrum, the first breast milk let down by cows and other animals after birthing. The milk is loaded with antibodies, vitamins, and a morphine-like substance, and cleans out the intestines of the young.

Find: To give birth, as in "Our cat found kittens last night—in the hall closet."

Biddy: Baby chicken.

Comes off: When a hen hatches biddies she comes off her nest.

Diddles, dibs: Biddies.

Settin' of eggs: A clutch of 12 to 15 eggs, depending on heft of the broody hen.

Steal nests: Broody hens do it.

Yard egg: An egg laid on the premises but outside the henhouse, as in a fence jamb.

Bird minders: South Carolina rice field hands engaged to frighten off, in autumn, migrating bobolinks, or rice birds.

Tow sack, tow bag, croaker sack: A burlap bag used initially to contain fertilizer and subsequently used for cotton pickin', leaf haulin', sack races, and chicken stealin'. Professor Hans Kurath, in *A Word Geography of the Eastern United States*, says that "tow sack" and "biddy" are "real Tarheelisms."

Natured: Something come by naturally, as in "This river bottom is right natured for corn," and "Steers are sort of natured like horses—they work like horses," and "Snakes are natured that way, and that's why a snake is a damned snake."

Faulty: Wormy, as an apple that fell early to the ground.

Dry house: A building with furnace similar to those in tobacco barns and used to dry sliced apples. Most times, apple slices are dried on rooftops.

By the dry month: A farm hand who works by the dry month is paid for working twenty-four days. No pay when it's too wet to plow.

Rabbit hunting: The dishonest practice of some tobacco warehousemen of reselling piles of tobacco at the expense of farmers and tobacco companies. This comes about by warehousemen knowing what grades of tobacco are desired and, on finding piles of desired tobacco that sold lower than expected, paying the farmer as scheduled but changing the ticket—the record of sale—and billing the tobacco company at the going and higher price.

Pinhooker: A free-lance tobacco buyer, a speculator, who finds bargains in piles of tobacco on warehouse floors, and then reworks and resells them for profit. The name comes from putting a safety pin in the sales tag, signifying that warehouse workers should leave the tobacco be.

Rat: A pile of tobacco bought and subsequently judged as not being up to snuff.

Meddering: Gathering hay from a mountain meadow.

Lassy b'ilin': The boiling of cane and sorghum juices.

Ship stuff, shorts: By-products in the milling of wheat. Once relegated to chicken and hog feed, they now are favored for human consumption. The term refers to ease of shipment of the lightweight and undemanding goods.

Down row: The row of corn knocked down by the team and one-horse wagon in harvesting.

Farmin' in the woods: Manufacturing moonshine, or illicit, booze.

Blockade: Moonshine whiskey.

Blockader: An illicit distiller; a moonshiner.

Run: A moonshiner makes a run when he completes a single distilling operation—when he fills, or charges, his still pot with the proper amount of fermented mash and converts the mash into booze. In the final stage of distilling and when condensation commences, the initial trickles of high-proof booze that come from the worm, or condenser, are "first shots."

Stash: Illegal booze stored in bushes and vacant structures.

Low-bush lightnin': Moonshine stashed in bushes for safe-keeping.

Trading with Nancy: Buying moonshine likker.

Cut down: Destroy an illegal distillery, usually using axes and dynamite.

Slider: A pint whiskey bottle—it can be slid across a counter.

Roller: A fifth of whiskey—usually round and can be rolled across a counter.

Tickler: A flat pocket flask.

Bat wing: A short pint of whiskey; fourteen ounces.

Bootlegger's pint, short row of corn: Twelve ounces.

Old hog: One-half pint South Carolina dispensary whiskey bottle, the one with the embossed palmetto.

Born: A half-pint of whiskey.

Methodist measure: Short. The allusion to short measure reflects on Methodists, who sprinkle in baptism, as opposed to Baptists, who favor the deep dip.

Stopper: A drink measure. This from glass stoppers in old decanters that served as shot glasses as well as bottle stoppers.

Barrel dogger, steamer, roller, sweater, burner: One who steams used whiskey barrels, fresh from legal distilleries, to extract whiskey that had been absorbed in the aging process in the white oak barrel staves.

Sanctum sully: Whiskey that drinks mighty easy.

There ain't no bad whiskey—some's good, some's better: Some whiskey would draw blisters on a rawhide boot, or cause a she-baby-bullfrog to spit in a whale's face. And some moonshine is so good you can taste the feet of the gal what hoed the corn it was made out of.

# How's the Weather?

*It's true, Lord, that we didst ask for rain. And it's true that we didst ask for no flimsy flamsy drizzle-drazzle, but for a gully washer and a trash mover. But, Lord, this is ridiculous.*
> —*A North Carolinian who prayed for rain and got a deluge*

The coldest time since the *Crissie Wright* come ashore: Sailors froze in the spray when the *Crissie Wright*, a schooner out of Boston, was grounded on North Carolina's Shackleford Banks, January 11, 1880.

Hog-killin' weather: Cold enough to butcher hogs without the fresh meat spoiling.

Cold enough to freeze the stink off shit: A whole overcoat day.

Turned off: Changed—the weather switched to hot or cold.

Troubly: Cloudy.

Weather breeders: Warm spells in the midst of cold.

Falling weather: Unsettled. When smoke from kitchen chimneys drifts to the ground, rain or snow is indicated.

Kitchen-settin' weather: When it's cold as kraut. Sauerkraut in crocks of brine stored in Appalachian smokehouses, basements, and root cellars is cold as a witch's tit in a brass bra.

Faired off: The weather cleared. It's faired off when the weather is cleared up.

A fair morning: A lovely day ahead.

Airish: When wind blows hard and cold enough to freeze whitecaps in the slop jar.

Peelin' the green: Wind blowing hard enough to peel bark from trees.

Pinchy: Biting cold.

Blue cold: Cold, and blue as a possum's balls—that is, cerulean.

Fresh: A fresh morning is cold, windy, raw and often a whole overcoat colder than the day before.

A good season: A long slow rain; a sizzle sozzle. Good seasons soak into the soil and pearten up crops. Much water in hard rains runs off and hardly gets beneath the surface.

Sizzle sozzle, sizzly sozzly, drizzle drazzle: A good season. From a prayer by Uncle Billy Duke, of the Duke University generation of Dukes: "O Lord, send us some rain. We need it. But don't let it be a gully washer. Just give us a sizzle sozzle."

# How's the Weather?

Mizzly: Less precipitation per hour than in a sizzle sozzle.

Circuit rider's weather: Sleety and stormy in the worst way. The itinerant preacher made his rounds regardless of weather, and remembered it most often as bad.

Gully washer, trash toter, fence lifter, chunk mover, goose drownder, frog strangler, clod buster: A hard rain.

Collards sitter, nubbin stretcher, toad floater, turd floater: A pour down.

Cod deep: A hard shower; a tol'ably heavy rain up to one's.

A power of rain: When it rains pitchforks an' yearlin's.

Like a cow pissin' on a flat rock: Big drops and close together in a sudden downpour.

Close cloudy: An overcast right-down-to-the-ground day.

A cold fish of a day: Damp; dark; chilling; miserable.

Gray day: Overcast.

Giffy: Cloudy and damp.

Snibblin': Dark; cloudy; rainy.

Drearisome: Gloomy; very dreary.

Mokey: Hazy; foggy.

Weathered: What it did when there was rain, snow, sleet.

Skift of snow; skirmish of snow: A light snowfall; a flurry.

Gipsen snow: Same as above.

Tramp snow: Term for an elusive "pat, pat" sound in fireplaces when fires are low; a sign of falling weather.

Calling the snow: When a wood fire in a fireplace pops, sputters, crackles, snow will follow within three days.

Dutch weather prophet: One who predicts weather by examining goose bones. The term refers to residents of the Dutch Fork section of South Carolina, between the Saluda and Congaree rivers, who were proficient in this sort of thing.

Biscuit weather: Snowy.

Thick as a featherbed: A description of snow and fog.

Groundhog's makin' coffee: When patches of mist rise to treetops. Dr. Cratis Williams has told me that groundhogs frequently emit puffs of steam, or what folks take for steam. This is when they are frightened of a sudden and dart into their holes. Maybe it's a smoke signal of warning.

Spring fresh; big fresh; stout fresh: A freshet; a sudden heavy rain, hard, quick and overflowing.

Makin' up: Storm clouds forming.

Thunderin' aroun': Storm clouds and thunder.

Thunder flurry: Thunder gust.

Corn wagon: A summer thunderhead.

Nubbin killer: Thunder. Thunderstorms frequently blow down stalks of growing corn, thus damaging the young ears.

Draw rain: Attract rain. To make rains come within three days, hang a dead black snake on a fence or in a tree. "The sky's been puckered all day," the Outer Banks native said, "but it ain't commenced to rain yit."

The devil's beatin' his wife: Said of a warm spring rain while the sun shines. Raindrops are the wife's tears.

Gone back to get another armful: Said of a lull in intermittent showers.

Dry weather shower: A shirt-sleeve rain; not enough rain to lay the dust; a smidgen; a mizzle.

# How's the Weather?

Oklahoma rain: A dust storm.

Pea ripper: Hot enough to bust open peas on the vine.

Corn twister: When it's hot as a burnin' stump.

Hot enough to fry spit: Hot as the hinges of hell—and that's about seven times hotter than ordinary fire.

Hot as floogies: Hot as a depot stove; floogies, or floozies, are promiscuous females.

Puthery: Sultry.

Sweaty months: July, August, September.

Corn's a-rubbin: Dry weather.

The river's so low we're haulin' water to it: It's so low, when a catfish swims upstream he's got a bullfrog going' ahead, takin' soundin's.

Toid's so hoigh the sherkes come in an' et me collards: High water in North Carolina's Carteret county. "Hoigh toid" is what smartasses say when they try to mimic coastland accents.

Slick ca'm: A calm sea.

Dish ca'm: Water as flat and calm as a dish.

Fish-eye slick: A ca'm ca'm.

Ca'med out; ca'med down: Calmed.

Mullet blow; mullet shift: Wind from the northeast with a corresponding drop in temperature, causing jumping mullet to school, or congregate, in North Carolina's Bogue and Core Sounds.

July galey: A long ago gale in July that separated a portion of North Carolina's Outer Banks, forming Hatteras and Ocracoke islands.

August gust: Intermittent and light rains in late July and early August, preceding hurricane-breeding weather.

Spell: There are assorted spells of weather—wet, dry, hot, cold—and none are brief.

Cold snap: A short span of cold weather. There are no wet, dry, or hot snaps.

Catbird winter: A cold pinching spell at about the time catbirds return hereabouts from their wintering places. Other winters associated with spring-bringing cold spells are named for and come when blooms are on dogwoods, blackberries, locusts, sarvice, gooseberries, and redbuds.

January thaw: A warm spell and just right to put in, or plant, early cabbage, onions, and greens.

# There's Another Way of Saying It

*Scenography of the Celestial Regions, being a treatise on Diosphantasmegorology and Ontology, or a full Diosphantasmeologic Pantography of the Supermundane Domain. The Origin of Men, of Language, and of Scripture; the Cause of Creation and Life and Death; the formation of Time and Eternity; and the reasons why it is natural to die, &C. By M. J. Custard.*

> —The title of a book in progress,
> as reported in the Natchez
> (Mississippi) Free Trader 'way
> back yonder

I'd plow her to death just to see her walk: Admiration, triple distilled.

Buy on tick: Charge it.

Charge it to the dust and let the rain settle it: Write it off.

I'm sittin' in the amen corner: I agree with you.

Lick that calf again: Clear the confusion; tell it to me once more, and slowly.

I chew my tobacco just once: I've spoken my piece; I've done said it.

Threshing the straw: Repeating; spelling it out again.

Come in to the books: Classes are about to commence.

Not much schoolhousing: Little schooling.

School breaking: School closing; commencement.

When school kept: When school was in session.

Greasy poke: Second best. From a bag or sack used previously for toting oily or greasy materials.

Greasy door family: One that's just killed hogs.

Ain't no never mind: The hell with it. Forget it.

It cut no squares with me: Made no impression. The cutting of squares refers to quilting; squares of cloth are pieced to make quilts.

I don't care about it a bit more'n spit in the fire: Indifferent.

No ham and all hominy: All work and no play.

More bubble gum than I can chew: More ground broke up than I can tend; more problems than I can say grace over.

That ain't no hill for a stepper: It's no problem for one who knows his business.

Comers and goers: Tourists; the summer complaint.

Comers and stayers: Visitors who wear out their welcomes

and leave only when assigned chores such as sloppin' the hogs.

Come heres: New folks in the neighborhood.

Belongers: Natives.

Revenants: People in ghost stories who return from the world of the dead.

Zombie: A snake god and a spell, from voodoo cults; a corpse reanimated by supernatural power. Harnett Kane writes that revenants are simple ghosts "—harmless creatures most of the time, with nowhere to go, roaming about a graveyard, fiddling among the orange trees, or trying, poor things, to sample a few oysters on a reef that they had once dredged. A zombie is worse, a ghost with something on his mind. When you paddle through a swamp and see a zombie staring at you, get out of that place."

A high lonesome: A drinking spree.

Celebrate: Achieve an exuberant state by indulging in strong drink.

Pinder boilin': A euphemism for a cocktail party in precincts of South Carolina's Grand Strand where the Moral Majority underground makes waves. Pinders are peanuts and usually on hand at cocktail parties.

You pulled the wrong sow by the ear: You got the wrong dog by the tail; you woke up the wrong passenger; you're barking up the wrong tree; wrong number.

The Lord willin' an' if the clothes line don't fall down: If h'it's so I kin, I will.

If nothing breaks or comes untwisted: Same as above.

If the creek don't rise and stop the mailman: Ditto.

Complected: Complexioned.

Imitates: Resembles; favors, as in "He imitates his pappy 'roun' the eyes."

Favorance: Resemblance.

Spittin' image: Said of someone in the spirit and image of a parent who had died. Joel Chandler Harris, Jr., said the term is Southern black in origin and has nothing to do with saliva. I refer the reader to about three inches of type in the *Morris Dictionary of Word and Phrase Origins*, p 538. Harold Wentworth is named here on the side of *spirit and image*, because the Southern "r" is often indistinct. Thus *spirit* is often produced as a sort of *spee-it* and shorter, as in *spit.*

Got his beauty struck: Had his picture taken by a man going through the country in a likeness wagon.

Most speaking: Natural enough to eat pie, said of a portrait that could almost speak at you.

Don't get cross-legged; don't get your dander up: Don't get your ass in a sling; don't get your wires crossed or your signals mixed; don't get upset without understanding the situation.

Shoe leather express: Pick 'em up an' lay 'em down.

That'll pass ever'thang but a fillin' station: What a gas guzzler will do.

Captain of a land packet: Driver of an ox cart.

Three hots and a flop: Three meals and a bed.

He's jumpin' somebody: He's giving a quick charge to somebody's automobile battery via a jumper, or booster, cable.

All right for a sittin' but not for a spell: For occasional use only.

Shackly; shackledy; shackelty: Ramshackle.

Sanitary step-aside: A wall urinal. The term was popularized by W. Kerr Scott, a North Carolina governor and United States senator.

Necessary: A euphemism for outhouse, backhouse, gardenhouse, craphouse, shithouse, jackhouse, privy, facility, outside plumbing.

> There was a feller named McBryde
> who fell in a two-holer and died.
> Along came his brother
> who fell in the other.
> And they were interred side by side.

Daughtered out: No more daughters available for marriage.

Hated out: The reason one left a community.

Out the light: Extinguish the light.

Invited not to come: Excluded. When bugs have a party they don't invite chickens. The phrase "invited not to come" was first brought to light and public print by W. C. Heinz, a sportswriter, in a relay from Roy Harris, a former professional heavyweight boxer of Cut and Shoot, Texas.

Leavin' out: Ain't stayin'.

Haul good: Travel, as "I don't haul so good no more."

Don't cut your foot: Watch that you don't step in cow dung.

Take the slack out of his rope: Defeat him; place him at a disadvantage.

Hind part forward: Ass over teacup.

Oklahoma credit card: A hose to siphon fuel from somebody else's tank.

Got what the bear grabbed at: Nothing.

Fertigue-inest: Most tiring.

Foller speakin', foller talkin': The ability of lawyers, preachers, and political figures to sound off in public.

Grunt: Attract alligators by imitating their calls.

Set a spell on: Bewitch.

Wet ass, hungry gut, an' nary a scale: Fisherman's luck.

Gumshot: Slingshot.

Gravel flipper, juvember: Beanshooter.

A rich man's war and a poor man's fight: 1861–65.

Seed corn of the South, seed-corn cadets: Teenagers enrolled in Confederate military service in the Late Unpleasantness. Jefferson Davis said that putting youngsters into service was like "grinding seed corn."

In on the play: In on the deal; to have inside information.

Everybody's in the same pew: It's all set and organized.

Blew his doors off: Passed in a hurry, as Junior Johnson used to do in stock car racing and in runnin' likker.

Keep his plow moving: Keep him busy.

She drove her ducks to a bad market; drove her ducks to a poor puddle: She fell in with the wrong crowd and went to the bad. Said a grandmother of a headstrong lass: "If she burns her ass, let her set on the blister."

A fine howdy-do: An embarrassing or troublesome state of affairs.

Tree his squirrel: Stump him on a problem or predicament.

He was put on the hog train: He was misled.

In a bad row of stumps: In trouble; in an unpleasant situation.

He's where the dogs won't bite him: He's in prison.

# There's Another Way of Saying It

Not a tater in the patch: Rejected; was refused a favor.

Turned down cold-footed: Same as above.

They ran his face: He got a bank loan without putting up collateral; he got a charactor loan.

Striking the street: Making a living on the street by panhandling, cadging, hustling.

Slick as a whistle: Slick as a smoothin' iron, as snot on a doorknob, as soap grease.

Slick as a button on a shithouse door: Slick as bark on a hen turd tree.

Get back to the chicken pen and start scratching: Return to the basics.

Shut up like a morning glory: Dejectedly silent.

Back and forth: Conversation.

An Unbiased Account of the War Between the States from the Southern Point of View: The title of a South Carolinian's unpublished manuscript.

Just as sure as a cat's got climbing gear: Right as rain; just as sure as God made little green apples.

I've seen too many frosty mornings: I don't stir aroun' early of a day any more.

I drank at the branch: I'm ahead of you and your story.

We're grinding corn: We're making progress.

Huckleberry over my persimmons: You've got a horse on me; you're one up; that's more than I can take; it's beyond one's knowledge, comprehension, or reach.

They don't shed their teeth: Said of families so inbred that certain characteristics prevail, generation upon generation.

Cheeped it: Told it.

Never said pea turkey: Failed to give information, or to invite one to some function, as "She lef' heah, I tell you, an' nevah said pea turkey.

Mind; call to mind: Recollect, as "I mind the time when wash-day was allus of a Monday."

Disremember: Forget.

Raise a bead: Bring to a head.

Store-boughten: Usually refers to whiskey made and sold legally.

Named: Mentioned, as "I seen him yesdiddy an' he nevah named it to me."

The beach is smoking: Wind-blown sand drifts and creates haze.

We didn't have a dog in that fight: We weren't involved.

Chew the bark off: Examine thoroughly; study it over.

Study out: Formulate, as in "God must to of put more time a-studyin' out oak trees than any other sort."

Done to a cracklin': Perfect. A cracklin' is what's left when lard is rendered—as you should know by now.

Cut your patchin': As you were; resume what you were doing. Patching refers to squares of cloth used to seat balls for firing in muzzle-loaded firearms.

As strong as horse piss with the foam farted off: Like coffee so strong it'd swim a wedge p'int fo'most.

That's a new wrinkle on my horn; a new ring on my horn: You are telling me something new or novel; a new trick; a smart dodge.

Lay out of school: Play hookey.

The truth and the backbone of the whole matter: The gospel truth.

Saw gourds; saw logs: Snore

Crank the car: Start the car.

Boot: A car trunk.

Spoke mighty sharp: Spoke sharply.

So dry he had the rattles: A man with a thirst.

Squared off even: Even Stephen.

Stiff as a preacher's prick: So hard a cat couldn't scratch it.

Brush breaker: A pioneer, one who has "broken a right smart chance of brush."

I didn't catch his hat: He dated somebody else.

Sweet talk: Flattery; honeyed words.

Glad-eyed: Enticed.

Shooting at the hump: Pretending, or doing something halfway right. The term comes from the hunting of buffalo: A shot at a buffalo's hump is worthless—no vital parts there—and the proper shot is just after the foreleg.

Misery whip: A crosscut saw. When a crosscut saw buckles while in use, it is said to fold, and when it folds, it whips violently as it regains its shape.

Ride the saw: Make somebody else do the hard work, the dirty work, while you pretend to bear your share of the load. The term comes from using a crosscut saw: You act like you pull with vigor, but you really coast, as in going through a revolving door on somebody else's push.

"Son," Uncle Terrapin said, "I don' min' yoh ridin', jus' don' drag yoh feets."

Brought on: Imported accessories such as cookstoves and pump organs.

Heap endurabler: Lasty, with permanence, as a spring from which water flows in a right smart trickle.

Out-doin'est: Sturdy; resilient; a remarkable survivor.

Body modest: You don't show everything you've got.

Short-tailed rooster: An adolescent male who has discovered girls and has a driver's license; one between hay and grass.

Shirttail boy: A tad.

Eatin' his salt: Enjoying one's hospitality, as "Bob Ford kilt Jesse James an' all the time he was a-eatin' of Jesse's salt."

A good stagger at it: A good try.

Have a whack at it, take a stab at it: Work at something that is bothersome or where others have failed.

Spilled the beans: Told it all, brother.

On a knife edge: In a precarious position; in a bind; in a tight.

The hair is in the butter: It's a delicate situation.

It was a sour tit but he sucked it: Anything my dog trees, I'll eat.

Hush mouth: Hush money.

Chips and whetstones, chips and grindstones: Odds and ends; payment in goods rather than cash. Two quilt patterns are named "chips and whetstones." One resembles four crowns joined with a cross, or an "X," and also resembles cogs, as in a pocket watch with broken teeth. The other resembles a mariner's compass, but the device in the center is square instead of round.

No bigger than the little end of nothin' whittled down to a fine point: Insignificant. Wilson Mizner, sometime Floridian, described the second husband of a rich widow as a "hole in the atmosphere."

That takes Billy's horns smooth off to his skull: That beats all; that takes the cake.

Shoot me for a billygoat: I'll be damned; I'm a monkey's uncle.

That's a heifer on my haslet: Same as above. "Haslet" means viscera.

Naw you ain't: An expression of astonishment or disbelief, meaning "You don't say?" or "Do tell?" or "Sho nuff?"

I wish to my never: An exclamation over something that is downright amazing.

That takes the rag off the bush: A statement of absolute astonishment or approval; to rant and rave and carry on. A rag removed from a bush signifies that one has found a lover or is engaged. Wash rags are often left on bushes to dry, and only a low person would steal one.

That puts the tassel on the cap: It's the icing on the cake; it beats all.

That caps the stack: Same as above.

Wouldn't that cock your pistol?: Wouldn't that light a fire under your tail?; wouldn't that surprise you? Some prudish or mock-modest persons would "rooster" pistols, the word "cock" being thought indelicate in some circles. That's why "John donkey" also is a euphemism.

John donkey: Jackass.

That beats cock-fighting: That surpasses anything yet—hen's a-pacin' or mules a-flyin'; it's too improbable or extraordinary to be true.

Past strange: Stranger than strange.

Sinker: One that a Louisiana lawyer for the defense wants on a jury—one who'd vote for acquittal.

Hindersome: In the way.

Fotched on: Outlandish; said of something to be resented or distrusted.

Ins and outs: The full particulars; the straight of things.

She's a-teasin' the cat: She's spending a penny; she's in the gardenhouse. Translate "cat" as pussy and "gardenhouse" as outhouse.

He looked at me like I was a bottle of stale piss: Like I was worse than dirt on a stick.

The ox is in the ditch: An emergency has arisen, requiring top priority.

Signify, syndicate: Intimate; insinuate; discuss; gossip.

Turn the truth: Modify the evidence to suit one's convenience.

Return an answer: The favor of a reply is requested.

I've read behind him: One is familiar with what another has written.

Scripted down: Recorded in writing.

Clean cat fur: Fully as represented; above reproach; the real McCoy.

Up to snuff: Standard; good as advertised; performance tested; worthy of Good Housekeeping Seal of Approval.

When the rabbit hollered and the peter bird sang: Fish and game were plentiful.

You've got the saw by the wrong tree: You ain't tellin' it right.

Couldn't see through a ladder: Drunk; grogged to the gills.

Shot in the neck: Same as above.

A-walkin' in a foggery: Disoriented.

Scat: Gesundheit; God bless you. Sneezing babies and cats that go "pfth" sound the same. A sneeze of man-sized proportions will scatter cats four ways from Sunday.

Georgia buggy: Wheelbarrow.

Sitting in the catbird seat: Sitting pretty, as a batter in baseball with three balls, no strikes and the bases loaded, or a poker player with an ace up and two in the hole. The term was popularized by Red Barber, Floridian, when he did baseball broadcasts for the Brooklyn Dodgers in the forties and fifties.

Preach over his likker: Pronounce moral judgment when one is not qualified to throw rocks.

The sort of folks that John the Baptist spoke about: Snakes in the grass. Matthew 3:7, Luke 3:7.

If you need somebody to push you in the creek, lemme know: If I can do you a turn, a favor, just ask.

Christmas is right in my mouth: Christmas is so close I can taste it.

Christmas has jumped the fence: The Thanksgiving Day parade just went past.

Brought his saddle home: Turned the tables on him.

You can hear her three fields off: She's loud of mouth.

Put the spit on the apple: End the argument.

Put that in your pipe and smoke it: The wrap-up statement of triumph after delivering irrefutable evidence or opinion in half-friendly debate.

If we'd a-knowed you was a-comin' we'd a-baked a cake: Welcome.

Scunnered: Disgusted.

Belittle: To disparage; to deprecate. "Belittle" was coined by Thomas Jefferson. It was disliked by James Fenimore Cooper, who also opposed "oppose," "advocate," "deputize," and "boss"; he asked Noah Webster to help put down these "slang" terms.

Anglophobia: Dislike of England and things English. Another Jeffersonian coinage.

Reel-footed: Club-footed.

Flinder: Break into small pieces.

Spot cards: A deck of playing cards.

Roses: A poker hand—two fives, two tens—named for a variety-store chain, Roses, based in North Carolina.

Dallas to Fort Worth: A poker hand—three tens—for the thirty miles that used to separate Dallas and Fort Worth.

Damn nasty oath: Corruption of the "Amnesty Oath" required of losers in the Second War of Independence.

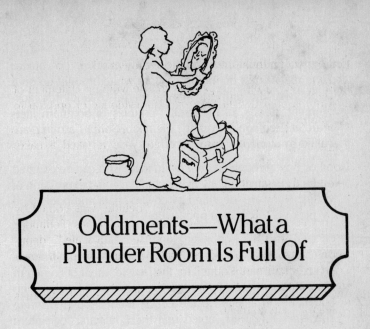

# Oddments—What a Plunder Room Is Full Of

*You come on up out from back down in under there, or I'll whup ever' bit of hide from offen yore back.*

> —Ms. Mona Whitt Williams of Blaine, Kentucky, to a youngster hiding under a kitchen table

Redneck: One of conspicuously Southern, rural, or small-town origin. The term originated in Mississippi in the later nineteenth century to describe poor white subsistence farmers, sharecroppers, and tenants. They had red necks from working long hours in the fields.

Grit, grits: Hillbilly, mountain boomer, cracker, po' bukra. *Time* magazine's definition: "A poor white brought up on a Depression dirt farm in Georgia, fearful of landlords, government, floods, of life itself." Courses in Southern literature at Clemson University, Clemson, South Carolina, are called by students "grit lit."

Good ol' boy: A rough and ready fun lover who can be counted on for most anything involving challenge and expression of virility. Many are identified by cowboy hats and boots, and by pick-up trucks equipped with CB radios, fishing rods, and fire-arms.

Coon-ass: A good ol' boy in Cajun country. James Domengeaux, Chairman, Council for the Development of French in Louisiana, or Conseil pour le Development du Française en Louisiane, in a letter to the editor, Baton Rouge *Morning Advocate,* July 1981, noted that the Louisiana legislature had recently condemned use of the term "coon-ass" in application to Acadians or Cajuns. He wrote further:

The Legislature concluded that this word came into use after World War II by the accidental commingling of sound with the French noun *conasse.* The word *conasse* is used in French to designate an ignorant or stupid person, a prostitute without a health card, a man who does stupid things or a grossly stupid person. . . .

The Acadians have suffered great indignities throughout history. We have virtually lost our language, our heritage and our culture. This tragedy, in part, has been self-inflicted. Can it be that this inferiority complex is continuing? Can this complex perhaps be the reason why certain of our prominent people, including Ron Guidry, a former governor and two Acadian Congressmen (who identified themselves as "Coon-ass Congressmen" while visiting the president) continue to use this offensive, degrading, linguistically illegitimate term?

If we are to save our language, culture and heritage, we must regain our pride and confidence in ourselves. The *derrière du chaoui* comparison cannot accomplish this.

Cracker: A native of Georgia and of Florida. Prior to westward migration, early livestock drovers and herdsmen in the Southern states controlled their walking stock by extravagant use of long whips—whips that cracked with the sharp report of rifle shots. These drovers and herdsmen—these crackers—were forerunners of latter day cowboys.

From drovers with bullwhips there was a progression in the language to "bullwhackers"—drovers who handled teams of oxen hitched to freight wagons. Their bullwhips usually had lashes a dozen feet long, and an expert with a bullwhip could flick the ear of a lead ox or mule, or a cigarette from the mouth of a girl performing in a sideshow. A duel between bullwhackers using bullwhips was a "lap-jacket."

North Carolinians are Tar Heels (two words) and once were known as Tar Boilers, both nicknames pertaining to the state's early prominence in the naval stores industry. Kentuckians have been known as Corn Crackers and Briars. West Virginians have also been known as Briars, the name, in the case of each state, pertaining to briar patches, indicating a rustic background. Mississippi has been known as the Mudcat State, for catfish, and Georgians also are known as goober-grabbers.

South Carolinians are Sandlappers—another word for clayeaters. Once a term of derision, the Sandlappers tag now is a badge of honor.

Virginians are known as Sorebacks, and some may take umbrage at being so identified. They won the distinction during the Civil War when a Virginia regiment found too many Yankees opposing them and, with prudence displacing valor, the troops hugged the ground. North Carolina troops, ready and willing to fight, attacked over the bodies of the prostrate FFVs — First Families of Virginia — and carried the day. Or so they say.

Ishy; free issue: Free blacks and their immediate offspring. Dr. Paul D. Escott says of "free issue":

> Its origin predates the Civil War. It can apply to the offspring of a white and black union, but I have also seen it applied to free blacks, both of whose parents were black (or mulatto). I suspect that in early days all the children of a free black couple were regarded as "free issue," since the issue of a free woman's womb was also free."

Dr. John Hope Franklin writes:

> As I understand it, "free issue" was a term used *after* 1865 to refer to Negroes who were free *before* the Civil War. It had nothing to do with miscegenation, though there were some free blacks of mixed ancestry. The distinction, as one put it, was between those who were born free and those who were shot free.

Blue-gum: A black man or woman with blue gums instead of pink. In folklore a blue-gum is revered as an adept conjurer, and also one with a poisonous and often fatal bite.

Sho-nuff: Genuine, as a "sho-nuff Yankee."

Seldom ever: Hardly ever.

My hind foot: The hell you say.

In a pig's eye; in a pig's ass: Same as above.

I swan, I swannie: Euphemisms for "I'll swear," "I'll be damned," "I'll be kiss my ass."

What the Sam Hill?: What the hell is going on?

Take time about: Alternate; take turns; spell off. Oysters do it— they change sex.

Gaumy, gaumed up: In disorder; soiled; gummy, like a child eating peanut brittle.

Begalmed: Same as above.

Thronging: Crowded with much back-and-forth, as a county seat town when big court is in session.

Free: Freely, as "I done et so free o' fish my stumick rises an' falls with the tide."

Do it up brown: Do to perfection, as something cooked to a turn.

Georgia costume: A collar and spurs. Senator James Murray Mason of Virginia appeared on the floor of the United States Senate on the eve of the Civil War, wearing a homespun suit to dramatize Southern nationalism. When President Lincoln heard of it, he said, "If that's the plan, they should begin at the foundation, and adopt the well-known 'Georgia costume' of a shirt collar and a pair of spurs."

 Mason later was involved in the celebrated "Trent affair" when he and John Slidell, en route to Europe as commissioners for the Confederate states, were taken from the British ship *Trent* by Federals and imprisoned.

To contrary: To fret or worry someone.

Light: Quit buzzin' aroun'; quieten down; sit.

Hear tell: Understand, as "I hear tell that she don't keep her ankles crossed."

Abide: Tolerate. Usually one can't.

Slaunchways, sidegartlin': Slanchwise; antigodlin; slanting; on a diagonal; awry; askew; off the main track; out of square; out of plumb; cattercornered; cattywampused; hip-sheltered; crook-sided; slanchindicular.

Contrarious: Same as above.

I'm a great mind to: I'm inclined to.

Baitin' trouble: Asking for it.

Kindly: Sort of, as "Yours truly kindly suffers from ineffable laziness."

Gumption: True grit; sturdy; git-up-an'-go.

A-takin' on: Overly demonstrative, like some mourners and dogs that've treed a quarry.

Weak as pond water: Like some sermons and some booze.

Strong as new well rope: Opposite of above.

A strong article: Like blackberry brandy produced for home remedies.

A touch of the ardent: A strong article.

Backassed: Shoehorned, like crowding a small automobile with passengers to set a new mark for the *Guinness Book of Records*.

Cat's water: Gin. Corn whiskey and apple brandy of high proof often are mistaken for panther piss.

When you come down to it: When you get to the bottom line.

Might could; might should: It's possible, but not as I know of.

Horn in: Intrude.

Didn't go to: Didn't intend to.

Level best, dead level best: When you do your damnedest.

Don't split your britches: Don't over-exert; don't get riled up and show your ass.

A fine howdy-do: An embarrassing or troublesome state of affairs suddenly come upon. It's enough to harelip Abraham Lincoln.

That will set the hair: That will anger, surprise, frighten, or give one pause. The expression comes from butchering hogs in family farm operations. After being killed, the hogs are scalded in water heated to 135–140 degrees, depending on heft of the animal. This sets the hair—stands it on end—making it easier for one to scrape it from the carcass.

Set the hair, in cowboy parlance, means to ride a horse long enough to take out the meanness.

Pushed for; in a push: In need of; hard pressed.

Done done: Irrevocable as a word said, a putt missed, a toilet flushed.

Sure don't: The phrase sounds at first hearing like "sure do," but it's a mannerly "no," as in "Do you cash checks?"

Misfixed: Out of whack; in disrepair.

Church is out: That put the fat in the fire; you told it all, brother.

By his lights: By his standards, his way of thinking.

Smothersome; Cloying; suppressing. A virile man trapped in a household of simpering women in a week of high water is in a smothersome situation.

Jawed: Gabbled; gobbled; talked; prated.

Gabblement: An exhibition of the preceding.

Carry on: To be overconversational, emotional, as in "Law, but she carried on somethin' turble when he up an' lef' her— she sounded like she was 'bout to have kittens."

Laid off: Quit, as "He's laid off milk an' whiskey both."

High as a Georgia pine: Intoxicated.

Tie hack: A hewer of railroad ties.

Peep: Comment, as in "I don't want to hear another peep out of you."

Warn: Give notice to appear, like one notified to work on the local road or provide or pay for an acceptable substitute.

Trying to cut a big hog with a little knife: Working with inadequate equipment or under adverse circumstances.

Give out: Announce; acknowledge, as "Short-tail Bob is give out to be the bes' squirrel dog aroun' here."

Give out: Give up on, as "Clara Della give out on seein' you ag'in, so she up an' lef' out of here with a fruit tree salesman."

Norate: Spread the word. Usually gossip, not gospel.

Let on: Confide; pass the word quietly.

Made out: Communicated, often to deceive, as in "He made out that he thought a sight of her."

Mess with: Be involved or otherwise engaged in, as "Carbine Williams used to mess with likker. Tha's how come he got in trouble an' went to prison."

Choused: Cheated; defrauded; cosened; skinned; badgered; hazed; bedeviled.

A can of corn: An easy chore, like taking a pop fly.

Fresh out of: When you are just now and suddenly without something or other.

Antic: Playful. Clowns, calves, colts, kids are antic.

Rounder: A pistol; a card; a fun-loving person whose antics needn't surprise those in the know.

Hugging set to music: Dancing.

Tie her loose: Cast off; untie the mooring lines.

Hog wild: Superlative wildness. The expression comes from Colonial days when stock roamed free and there were no fence laws. George Washington was credited with more wild hogs than he could account for.

Will fotch a mighty figger: Worth a good askin' price.

Follow: Indulge in; desire, as in "He follers after women an' money."

Beatin'est: A superlative, as in "That's the beatin'est wish book I ever saw." Ranks with the New Englander's "finest kind."

Awfullest: Another superlative.

Readies: Hat, coat, purse and other items as must be assembled for a departure.

In the paint wagon: Where the drinking whiskey is.

Traipse: Meander; wander with little restraint.

Blackberried: Wandered off.

Shud, shed: Rid of, as "They got shud of their preacher."

'Way yonder: An advantage, a head start or more, as in "Women's got 'way yonder a better chance to get on in a dry goods store."

Jitney: A metal token and a public conveyance. Both uses are of Louisiana origin. The token was used in exchange for a ride on a jitney, or jitney bus, on which the fare was five cents.

Mind: Watch over; be heedful of; be responsible for, as one minds after a yard child, or a pot of chili on the stove, or a barbecuing shoat.

Go to the bad: Spoil; something that can happen to country hams and even to children who were raised up right.

Ripe enough to sprout legs and walk: Something that went bad.

Ganged around with: Ran with; associated with, as in "They ganged aroun' with Bonnie Parker an' Clyde Barrow."

Piled up with trash: Ganged around with a sorry crowd.

I've a mind to: I just might.

Scrooch up: Crowd together; swink up; shrink up.

Scringe: Cringe.

Runnin' the willers: Mississippi steamboat talk for threading slack water near shore.

Chiefing: What Cherokee Indians in western North Carolina posing for tourist photographs are doing for reward in coin of the realm—wearing Sioux war bonnets, headgear the old Cherokees never knew.

Show house: Movie theater.

Doin's: Ingredients; activities.

Common doin's: Plain.

Poor do: Inferior.

Doodly squat: Term of indifference, as in "I don't give a doodly squat if Woody Price does lose that fish."

Pure; purely: Absolutely; teetotally, as "He's done tol' a pure black lie, that's what he's done done."

Tell a story: Tell a lie.

Lie bill: A sworn statement giving lie to previous testimony.

Roaches: Minnows for fish bait.

Float: Launch; put a boat in water.

Mommix: Mess up; louse up.

# Oddments

Don't know whether to piss or go blind or shine shoes: In a dilemma.

I ain't studyin' you: Leave me be; I'm payin' you no mind.

Stomp clams; tread clams; toe clams: Find clams in shallow water by feeling them with your feet.

Sign clams: Discover clams by walking in clear, shallow water and watching for their signs: keyhole-shaped depressions made as they ingest and expel water.

Clurr: Clear or clean fish from a net.

Put a heap of store in; set a store by: Have faith in someone or something, as in "My mammy put a heap of store in Doctor Cullom."

Druthers: Choice; preference, as in "If I had my druthers, members of Congress could stay there no more'n a dozen years."

Liked: Lacked, as "He liked two weeks of making it to eighty-four years old."

Get the hang of it: Get the knack of it; determine how something operates.

As fair as your hand: As plain as day.

It don't make no never mind: It makes no difference; it never bothered me one cent in this world; it's no skin off my ass.

Gone to: Begun, as "It's gone to rainin' on the golf course a-ready."

Jubus; juberous: Dubious.

Tejus: Tedious.

Hent: Isn't.

As welcome as a collect telegram: Now don't that beat all?

Car shed: The shelter alongside tracks at railroad stations.

Store house: Grocery or dry goods store.

Like common: As always.

Pressing club: Predecessor of dry cleaning plants.

Brash: Brickly; brittle, as splits from white oak saplings that are hard to bend in bottoming chairs and in weaving baskets.

Pull hemp: Die by hanging.

Crow: Holler in derision.

Plugging: The pulling of teeth while you wait.

Dreadless: Doubtless.

Never turned a tap; never hit a lick: Never lifted a finger.

Work around: Work here and there for brief periods.

Broad spoken: Outspoken; one who uses coarse language.

Coarse: He who sings coarse sings bass; the same for him who basted. A tenor sings fine and a soprano sings shallow.

Sleepy gapes: Yawns.

As sure as gun's iron: Right as rain; as sure as Adam et the apple.

Own it: Confess it.

Fly blister: Mustard plaster.

Make: Mode, as in "This here make of livin' is too high-falutin' for me. They've got a outhouse in the house, an' they're a-cookin' outdoors."

Side-office lawyer: One who practices from an office adjacent to one's residence.

Gallimaufry: Hodge podge.

Buggit: Bundle; bindle; pack.

Take up: Assemble; collect; pick up; begin. One takes up stools or stands of waterfowl decoys, packs of beagles, and collection at church services. One also takes up projects such as whittlin'.

Take in: Assemble; collect; pick up; cater to. One takes in washing, boarders, roomers, and movies. Churches and schools take in when the last bell rings.

Fleshen up: Add weight.

Plump: Flat out; straightforward, without hesitation, as in "When he asked you, plump, if you would, what'd you tell him?"

Pass: A situation; a condition. On being faulted for upbraiding a political person of his own persuasion, Marse Henry Watterson, editor of the Louisville *Courier,* wrote, "Things have come to a hell of a pass when a man can't kick his own jackass."

Pass, passin': Pretend; to be taken for, as in "He passes to be her pappy," and "Rethelda? Why, she went up nawth an' she's crossed over—she's passin'."

Hincty, hinchy: Sporty patrons of sporting houses—white, overbearing, pompous, some wearing pearl-buttoned spats with revolvers to match. "God damn it, my guns are ivory handled," said General George S. Patton, Jr., alumnus of the Virginia Military Institute, class of 1907. "Nobody but a pimp from a cheap New Orleans whorehouse would carry one with pearl grips."

Gravels: Galls; irritates.

Jook, jook joint, jook house: An out-of-the-way oasis, a road-house, a pleasure house, a house of ill fame where men and women carry on—drinkin', dancin', singin', gamblin', makin' out.

Jooking, said Zora Neale Hurston, is playing piano and guitar as done in such resorts. Low down . . . blues . . . The music at first was from guitars—boxes, they were called. Then pianos, and player pianos, and talking machines. Finally, coin-operated phonographs—jook boxes as we know them today.

"Musically speaking," Ms. Hurston said, "the jook is the most important place in America. For in its smelly, shoddy confines has been born the secular music known as blues, and on blues has been founded jazz. The singing and playing in the true Negro style," she said, is jooking.

Ms. Hurston also said that a good jook singer must be able to "hoist a jook song from her belly and lam it against the front door. . . . She must also have a good belly-wobble, and her hips must, to quote a popular work song, 'Shake like jelly all over and be so broad, Lawd, Lawd, and be so broad.'"

A jook song reported by Ms. Hurston:

> Oh de white gal rides in a Cadillac,
> De yaller girl rides de same,
> Black gal rides in a rusty Ford
> But she gits dere just de same.

Jook should be spelled and pronounced *jook* to rhyme with *cook*. Ms. Hurston, born and raised in Florida where jooks flourished among palmettos and back streets, spelled and pronounced it that way. So did MacKinlay Kantor, another old Florida hand. "I'm damned if I spell the word j-u-k-e," he said. "It wasn't pronounced that way, and it still galls me to hear it or see it employed."

O.K.: Correct; approved. Archives of Sumner County, Tennessee, contain the first literary record of the term. In a document dated October 6, 1790, Andrew Jackson, Esq. "proved a Bill of Sale from Hugh McGary to Gasper Mansker, for a negro man, which was O. K." Some word-watchers say the "O. K." on the document was Jackson's poorly penned "O. R."—Ordered Recorded.

Dr. Robert Burchfield, editor of the *Oxford English Dictionary,* says that "O. K." came not from Jackson or, as some said, from Choctaw Indians, or from Italians, but from colloquial English: "orl (all) korrect."

Some kind of good: Of high degree; scrumptious; first rate; fit-nin'.

Larrupin' good: More than some kind of good, but who can you tell?

Cooter, slider, red belly, yellow belly: Terrapin; Pseudemys scripta.

Black-eyed Susan: A revolver.

Chapman Billies: Peddlers from the outside world doing business in eastern North Carolina. Anyone knowing the derivation, please advise.

Seat of work: Temporary employment of a journeyman tailor.

Texas: The upper or third deck of a Mississippi steamboat.

Texas tender: A waiter assigned to the Texas deck.

Flank the whole bottle: Achieve by strategy, by superb cunning.

The goose hangs high: Everything is looking up. This from the Southern sport of gander pulling. The gander was picked naked, greased (especially about the neck), and suspended head down with his feet tied to an overhanging tree limb. The object of dirt-road sports of the day was to ride a galloping horse, reach up, and grab and hold on to the goose.

See the elephant: Be disappointed after high expectations.

Acknowledge the corn: Admit losing an argument or a contest. A farmer went to New Orleans in the early 1800s to sell corn and potatoes. He fell in with gamblers who took him—they took his money and his two barges, one loaded with corn, the other with potatoes. When the gamblers came next day to collect, they found that the corn barge had sunk and that the farmer was determined to cut his losses. "I acknowledge the corn," he said, "but I'll be damned if you get the potatoes."

# Gardenin'—Front Yard and Back Yard

*The cornfield pea was the only faithful friend the Confederate Army ever had.*

> —General Robert E. Lee of
> Virginia

*One chilly evening in the early part of March the sheriff entered the county jail and, addressing the colored person who occupied the strongest cell, said:*

*"Gabe, you know that under the law my duty requires me to take you out of here tomorrow and hang you. So I've come to tell you that I want to make your final hours on earth as easy as possible. For your last breakfast you can have anything to eat that you want and as much of it as you want. What do you think you'd like to have?"*

*The condemned man studied for a minute.*

*"Mr. Lukens," he said, "I b'lieves I'd lak to have a nice wortermelon."*

*"But watermelons won't be ripe for four or five months yet,"*
*said the sheriff.*
*"Well, suh," said Gabe. "I kin wait."*
—*Irvin S. Cobb of Kentucky*

Kiss-me-over-the-gate; bush honeysuckle, mountain honey-suckle: Azalea.

Coon flower: Bloodroot.

Mile-a-minute: Kudzu.

Pretty-by-nights; peep-by-nights: Four o'clocks, flowers that bloom in late afternoon.

Whip-poor-will shoes: Lady slippers.

May pop: Passion flower.

Bride of the woods: Dogwood.

Farewell summer: Fall-blooming asters.

White and yellow Octobers: Chrysanthemums.

Gardenhouse lilies: Day lilies. Often planted about privies.

Feverfew: Summer chrysanthemums.

Fall roses: Zinnias.

Drowned men's fingers: The opening fistules of spider lily buds.

Rooster heads: Birdfoot violets.

Bammy gillyum: Balm of Gilead.

Touch-me-not: Pale jewel weed; snap weed.

Heart's a-bustin': Swamp dogwood; strawberry bush; spindle bush; arrowwood.

# Gardenin'

Possum bush: Pussy willow.

Love lies a-bleedin': Bleeding heart; luxuriant.

Sparrowgrass: Asparagus.

Peckerwaller: Dandelion greens.

Tendergreen: A young leafy vegetable.

Corner-of-the-fence greens: Purslane; pokeweed; sorrel; dandelion; plantain.

Okra: An annual cultivated for its green pods. which are used as the basis for soups and stews, especially gumbo. African slaves, it is said, brought okra seed to Louisiana, stowing it in their ears.

Pie plant: Rhubarb.

Quick: A plant that is alive and growing.

Garden sass; garden truck: Home-grown vegetables.

Sun power: What vegetables are filled with when gathered late in the day.

Moon power; star power: What vegetables are filled with when harvested early of a morning.

Umbrella tree: Chinaberry; magnolia tripetela.

Ti-ti, ty-ty: Buckwheat tree.

Scuppernong: A grape indigenous to the South Atlantic states. Ti-ti, scuppernong, pokeweed, squash, terrapin and racoon are words of Indian origin.

Shucky beans: Beans to be strung with needle and thread and hung for drying.

Arkansas strawberries: Dried beans.

Ozark dates, dog apples: Persimmons.

Sassafrak: Sassafras.

Bear grass: Coarse, tough grass; any of several species of yucca.

Laurel slick, laurel hell: Southern Appalachian mountainsides dominated by native rhododendron.

Pinders; goobers; goober peas; ground nuts: Peanuts. Peanuts are Brazilian in origin. They somehow got to Africa and were relayed to the southern states in slave trade. Professional word-watchers say that pinder, goober, okra, cush, cooter, zombie, hoodoo, voodoo, gumbo, poor joe, tote, jook, jazz, and pickaninny are among the few surviving contributions of African culture to Southern speech. The paucity of African words is attributed to aversion of whites to melding slave words with the language of the whites.

# Rasslin' the Devil

*Fellow sinners, I have preached to you. I have prayed for you, and often exhorted you to flee from the wrath to come; but not withstanding all this, here you now are as drunk as Billy be damned.*

*If you are determined to go to hell foremost, I am too good a shepherd to desert my flock in the hour of danger, and therefore will go with you.*

*Landlord, give us something to drink! Come on up, boys.*
> —*An unidentified parson in a combination grocery and groggery in Louisiana*

Scotch the preacher: Say "amen" now and then and grunt often during the sermon, thus indicating support of the preacher and the gospel offered.

Amen corner: The first pews in fundamentalist or evangelistic churches, usually in the right-hand corner facing the preacher; a place of privilege for elderly men who demonstrate piety by scotching the preacher.

Mourner's bench, anxious bench, anxious seat: Right in front of the preacher, indicating an anxiety to get salvation right away. The term first came to use in old Liberty Chapel, Greene County, Georgia. A revivalist by name of Stilth Mead packed the aisles with hysterical parishoners hurrying to find salvation. The soul saver could not speak with each one individually so he asked them to take turns in sitting in "the mourner's bench"—on the front row.

Basket meeting: Two or three days of religious services with "dinner on the grounds an' preachin' all around." So called because participants bring baskets of food.

Big meeting; protracted meeting; camp meeting: Religious programs lasting from two or three days to a week or more in late summer after crops have been laid by. Two sermons are heard daily, often with a visiting preacher and a visiting song leader. Hymns are h'isted heavenward, baptisms held in the river, courtships are developed, horses are traded. The blessed and the saved gorge themselves in basket dinners spread out on waist-high tables.

Line the song; line out; passel out: The song leader reads aloud the first two lines of the song to be sung, and the congregation sings them. The next two lines are read, then sung, and in this piecemeal fashion the whole song is sung.

Hymn h'ister: Song leader.

H'ist the tune; raise the tune: The song leader pitches the tune of the song to be sung.

Singin' an' shoutin' services: Church services wherein fervor is rampant.

Quick an' devilish music: It isn't traditional hymn singin' for sure, and it includes something of the Nashville beat.

Praise house: A place of worship on the sea islands of South Carolina and Georgia.

Preachin' takes up; preachin' takes in: Services commence.

Preachin' has broke: The service has ended.

Git limbered up an' goin' smooth: An essential for success among those who foller talkin'. When a preacher warms up to his job and gets the kinks ironed out, he can make either hell fire or salvation imminent.

Jerks: An orgiastic religious exhibition in which participants are seized in religious fervor and "struck down"—jerking and twisting in emotional spasms, shouting, sometimes collapsing unconscious and almost always awakening with sins forgiven and full of exhortations for others to join the throngs of sinners saved.

> MacKinlay Kantor told of a woman overcome by religious ecstasy—spraddled on the ground and out cold. When fellow worshippers sought to move and revive her, the preacher intervened: "No," he said. "Leave her lay where Jesus flang her."

> From other fervent services there are reports of women jerking their heads with such violence that their braided tresses snapped like buggy whips. And of true believers, stricken in ecstasy, running into woods, barking like dogs. Because rapturous excesses were likely at camp meetings, heads of households often barred their women folks from attending.

Jerkin' poles: Breast-high saplings, trimmed and smoothed and left standing amongst rustic pews in bush-arbor services.

> Jerkin' poles are stout anchors for those caught in the undertow of religious frenzy, something for them to

grab a-holt of, to jerk on, and to prevent them from tumbling away from the premises. An after-action report on a particularly wild service said the ground around the jerkin' poles looked like horses had been stompin' flies.

Comes through; pulls through: When one owns up to sins and professes religion. This emotional experience is usually followed by another: deep-dip baptism.

Got took down: Got religion.

Got hit by salvation: Same as above.

'Fessed religion: Ditto.

Quench the Spirit: Resist the Holy Ghost.

Put up: Pray; prayers are put up heavenward.

Lay in a distress: Bring charges; complain of the morals or misdeeds of another member of the congregation.

Notice: In fundamentalist churches a member is given notice, or invited, to appear before church authorities and the membership for disciplinary action.

Called on the carpet: One accused of sinning or un-Christian conduct usually is examined or sentenced while standing directly in front of the preacher and the congregation.

Churched, turned out: When one is voted out by the congregation or the ruling elders. The churched one is not allowed to return to church services for several months after repenting, or he must sit in a restricted area and forego communion. One may be churched for a multitude of counts of "un-Christian conduct." Fellowship may be denied for playing cards, but bingo is okay.

Sot aside, set aside; disfellowshiped; nonfellowshiped: Churched.

Foot-washin' Baptist: A fundamentalist, or Hardshell, Baptist with strict and rigid rules and a church service that includes foot-washing as part of the sacrament.

Voodoo, hoodoo: Mainly a black religion with rural roots, in which sorcerers create zombies and make magic by curse charms. Voodoo is derived from the African Ewe word *vodu,* meaning god, spirit; hoodoo is a variant spelling. Slaves brought the word to the Caribbean islands, and the French relayed it to New Orleans.

Bush arbor, brush harbor: Temporary structure covered with boughs for the holding of religious services in rural areas.

Scrippin' house, change house: Strippin' house where participants in riverbank baptisin's change to dry clothing.

Baptisin' day: The day when saints and sinners converge on river banks and grist mill ponds for deep-dip immersions.

Feeler: An assistant at baptisin's. His assignment is to scout stream and pond bottoms prior to the baptisin's, poking with a pole and feeling the way for the newcomers to Christ, so they won't bump into underwater obstacles or step in holes.

Lift the collection: Take the collection.

Poundings: Occasions wherein gifts, usually of food items weighing a pound or so, are given the new preacher.

Short-coat preacher: A lay or "called" preacher not influenced by seminary training.

Jimson-weed preacher: Same as above, but coarse, rustic and stubborn in belief. One described by playwright Paul Green as "a plowhandle sort of fellow."

Flatboat preacher: One who preaches and, on the side, sells booze.

# Old Country Conversation Pieces Revisited

*Ahm so tard ah feel like I been arnin' in muh bar' feet all day—*
*with no snuff.*

> —Overheard at the end of a long
> choir practice in a
> Birmingham, Alabama,
> Methodist church

*I just hunkered down, hit creeled, an' then hit poned up till I*
*thought hit was a-goin' to beal.*

> —An East Tennessean explaining
> his ankle injury: he squatted
> and turned his ankle and it
> swelled so much he thought
> the skin would split

Back back: That's what you do to properly maneuver an automobile in reverse gear. You don't back the car, or even back up. You back back. Also, if your car needs repair, you don't just drive it to the shop. You "carry" it by sitting in the driver's seat and driving it as you always do.

Do how, do what?: A question, usually a ploy, a stall to gain time to think up an answer to the previous question; means the same as "Run that one by me again."

Do tell, you don't say: An interjection to show interest.

Do don't: In South Carolina and Georgia it means do not.

How come?: Means the same as "why," but if asked by a grandchild it is appealing.

Sucking the hind tit: Often the situation in trying to draw to an inside straight flush, or in signing notes for friends and kin.

In the suck: To hold the bag; when you are taken in by somebody with no more chance of paying out than a one-legged man in an ass-kicking contest.

Owe the truth: Admit the truth.

Speak your piece: Say what you've got to say when you have a crow to pick with somebody.

That brings on more talk: It's a difficult question to answer.

Lay it back: Don't say whatever it is that you intend to say.

Lay it on: Give one a cussin'; tell it straight out; frail one.

Give him a time: Give him a fit; put his feet to the fire.

Settin' up to: Plotting.

All the go: Popular, as once were rumble seats, zoot suits, watch fobs, drop-stitch stockings.

It don't set good; hit don' seem jus' right: It doesn't win acceptance.

Ain't quite got it settled in my mind: Undecided.

On the back of: Also; in addition.

Sorry some: Distressed, as "I'm sorry some that I cain't light an' set."

On the up an' up: Improving; on the level; honest-to-God truth.

Hanker after: Lust for; crave; state of being horny.

Hurting for: In need of.

Tuk in an' did for: Was gulled; cheated; swindled; choused.

Skunned: Same as above.

Higher'n my pocketbook: It's unreasonable, like the cost of a plumber's services.

He'll put you on the ground: Endorsement of a lawyer who can spring you from the slammer.

Aim to: Intend to.

Waiting on: Waiting for.

Might can; might could: Maybe.

Tote: Some people tote, or carry, grudges, matches, messages, razors, firearms, tales.

  Many scholar-hours have been passed in trying to determine the derivation of the word "tote." Dr. Mathews, in *Some Sources of Southernisms,* apparently put the spit on the apple with this conclusion:

Now that Dr. Turner has completed his study of Gullah, there is no longer any reason for failing to recognize that this term is an Africanism brought to this country early in the seventeenth century. . . . The word occurs in Angola and in the Belgian Congo meaning "to pick up." . . . In the Ewe language of the Togo and Dahomey regions what is essentially the same word means to lift a load from one's head without help. In the Kimbundu and Umbundu languages *tuta* means to carry.

Must of: Must have, as in "Billy Graham must of got religion early."

Ought to of: Should have, as in "I ought to of gone to church more."

Public outcry: Public auction; sheriff's sale.

Hold to: Advocate; endorse, as in "Sam Jones didn't hold to daylight savings time and income taxes."

Abide: Tolerate; hold to.

Tie 'im to a tree 'n' run a wheelbar' 'roun' 'im: Advice on how to prepare a country boy for county seat vehicular traffic when big court is in session.

That's more like it: You're getting warm; you're solving the problem; you're close to the truth.

That's something; that's something else; that's something to see: Of an object or event that is superlative.

Better than: More than, as in "This here egg basket is better than fifty years old, I betcha."

Coursing the bees: Tracing wild honey bees on their path from bait to hive; you do this so you can rob the hive of honey. Bees travel a straight route from bait to hive—thus a beeline.

Peavine railroad: One with a rambling route—no beeline here—as in a mountain lumbering operation.

Coffee pot sawmill, peckerwood sawmill: A sort of one-gallus operation.

Tub mill: A small family-size grist mill, water-powered, geared to grind one or two bushels of corn a day.

Knocking weight: Altering scales to give short weight.

Play havance: Shoot marbles, or dinkies, for keeps.

Turn out: A display; as with a governor's inaugural.

Sociable: A party in a rural household; neighbors from all around knew they were invited when the hosts, late of the afternoon of the party, sent up a smoke signal by firing a brush heap.

A eatin': A party when you invite a lot of people to eat what you have spent all day a-cookin'.

Pipe's out: The party is over.

Clock dentist: One who repairs timepieces.

Coggled up: A right smart mess; one hell of a mess.

Run: Construct, as in "All the chimbleys you see aroun' here, I runned."

Cut a rusty: Pull a prank, a caper, to cut a shine or do something foolish or improper, as overturning the preacher's privy; to have a conniption fit; to outdo one's self; bedlam in a henhouse when a varmint intrudes.

Snake sheds: Skins of moulted snakes left hanging on smokehouse rafters or other quiet, dark and snakey places.

Hold out: Where you live, work, or meet.

Tote fair: Treat honestly; deal fairly and squarely.

Shorten the stick: Use unfair or foul means to gain advantage.

Got the shitty end of the stick, got the dirty end of the stick: Was had; was tuk in an' did for. The three terms preceding come from log-rolling. They were developed in days when trees were killed by girdling, then felled, then piled and burned. The logs were moved about by lifting them with stout sticks, or poles, two men to each, the log between them. So,

—Toting is fairly done when the weight is distributed evenly.

—When the stick or pole is shortened on one side, the load is uneven and unfair for the man on the short side.

—The shitty end of the stick resulted from horseplay, from coating one end of the stick or pole in ordure.

Play up to: Butter up; patronize.

Seldom ever: Hardly ever.

Heap o' times: There are occasions, as in "Heap o' times a-body'd fare better jist to say nothin'."

It'll answer: It will do for now.

Looked to see: Hoped for; expected; looked for, as in "I never looked to see Cliff split a ticket—he's allus been a straight party man."

Throw knives: Swap knives.

This knife's been to breakfast: It is dull.

Bunch up: Pool; consolidate, as when fox hunters gather with their pickups and hounds for a hunt and a feed.

The whole push: All in a group, crowd, as in "The whole push got after him to join the church."

Whole kit and caboodle; whole kit an' b'ilin': The whole wad—lock, stock and barrel.

Whole shebang: Same as above. "Shebang" originally meant a room, shop, tent, hut, cabin. The word was a corruption of the French *cabane* and was brought northward by Louisiana troops in the Civil War.

Lock, stock and barrel: the main units in rifles and shotguns.

All on one side: Like the handle of a vinegar, brandy, or molasses jug.

Wiggled an' wingled aroun': As with mountainside roads and trails.

Stomp down: Absolute, as "That's the stomp down truth, so help me."

Up against a stump: In a quandary.

In a split stick: In a bind; in a quandary.

String-halted: Restrained; restricted.

Make game of: Make fun of.

Make fiddle and fun: Same as above.

Cap: Ditto.

Guy: Josh; chide in a friendly putdown, like "How'd you get so ugly in jus' twenty-two years? Huh?"

Cut his comb: Humiliate him.

Out done: Hacked.

Hack; Embarrass; confuse; befluster; get the best of; make ill at ease.

Hawk: Same as above. To hawk also means to clear one's throat with a harsh palatal sound.

Pieded: Spotted, variegated.

Rolled the bed: Turned and tossed.

Horseback opinion: From where I sit without much information to go on.

Put up: Establish temporary quarters.

Put in: Unsolicited comment, as in "Nobody ast for nary bit of her put in."

Put the foot down: Lay down the law and leave nothing in doubt.

Lay off me: Leave me be.

Take care of: Avoid; watch out for, as in "Take care of that there dog a-layin' there in that there road."

Get on: Find employment.

Order off for: Make use of wish books and coupons.

A-comin' an' a-goin': Confusion.

Let in: Began, as in "It let in to rainin' 'bout an hour 'fore day."

What boots it?: What is the advantage, the profit?

> Alas! What boots it with incessant care
> To tend the homely slighted Shepherd's trade
> And strictly meditate the thankless Muse?
> —John Milton, *Lycidas*, lines 64–66

Blow: The amount one would register on a breathalizer, a device for measuring one's alcoholic content. One who blows more than .12 is usually knee-walkin' drunk.

Brew: Breed, as blow flies breed in fresh pork.

Belch back: Rebound.

Fill: A sufficiency, as in "I had my fill of that teacher."

A taste of the keg: Same as above.

Argify: Argue.

Sunburnt cake: Bois de vache; dried cow pies; prairie pancakes; cow chips; an old cow flop.

Out of: Without, as in "We're still out of a preacher."

Loafer around: Loaf; engage in aimless endeavors.

Messin' an mullin': Not involved in any worthwhile enterprise.

Pole around; progue around: What gangs of small boys do when they prowl and are up to mischief.

Progue: Prod; goad.

Projeckin'; gammetin': Assling; cutting up; frolicking; pranking; piddling.

Shoot the anvil: Wake up the neighborhood for miles around by exploding black powder in the blacksmith's anvil.

To properly shoot an anvil you remove it from the blacksmith's shop to the open, turn it upside-down and fill the hole in the bottom with black gun powder—a teacup is enough—and place another anvil or a heavy flat rock on top of the hole. Somewhere along here you lay a fuse or a trail of powder. You light the fuse and run unless, as Warren Wilhite said, you are willing to butt heads with an anvil in flight.

Shooting the anvils used to be customary on special occasions such as Christmas Eve, New Year's Eve, and election nights. Or whenever the blacksmith took a mind to celebrate.

Wasn't to no age: Wasn't old enough to marry, or get a driver's license, or buy whiskey from a poke store.

Poke store: Likker store, where purchases are put in brown paper pokes, or sacks, or bags.

Blood bank: Same as above.

Strike: Hit as in "How's that proposition strike you? Huh?"

Hard road: Paved road.

Cooter-backed road: An arched dirt road shaped in the manner of a terrapin's carapace and designed to shed water.

Corduroy road: A dirt road in which saplings and logs are laid crossways in muddy and gummy areas. Negotiating a corduroy road in a Model-T Ford would shake the liver and lights out of one—sort of like operating a pneumatic drill in an airport runway, or taking the first drink of just minted corn whiskey.

Law: Prosecute; call the sheriff.

Suspicion: Suspect, as "I suspicion he ain't a proper preacher; he's the law, for sure."

Bring the door: Close the door. "Shet the door" is a command; "shut the door" is a request.

Crack the door: Open the door a tad.

Fan the door: Keep the door open.

Hold your tater: Be patient.

Fetchin' stick: A long stick with a hook at one end. For use in grocery stores to jostle light items such as toilet paper and boxes of cereals from shelves higher than those in supermarkets.

Slack tub: A barrel of water in a blacksmith's shop, used to cool hot metal objects.

Quit suckin' eggs: When you've been exposed in some transgression or error, or have been brought to taw, you are supposed to quit suckin' eggs—to have learned from the experience.

Cow stomp: A shady place where cows take refuge from sunshine and heat and stomp their hooves to discourage flies.

Stompin' ground: Familiar precincts.

Some kind of: A degree of intensity, as "I'm some kind of sorry his ol' lady lef' with that there rainmaker."

By guess an' by golly: The formula by which many jackleg

carpenters, ditchbank blacksmiths, and shadetree mechanics build and repair.

Rack of eye: Chesapeake boat builders' term for building a boat without blueprints; the plans are in one's head. For a skipjack, the traditional formula is: The boom is the length of the boat; the mast is the length of the boat plus beam; the bowsprit is the length of the beam.

Right down: Downright; very, as in "Talk about nuclear waste disposal is right down serious, I tell you."

Knock you back: Give you pause; set you back on your heels. Fermented skimmin's left over in the manufacture of sorghum molasses will.

Lapped it up: Fell for it; took it all in; swallowed it.

Flat mail: Magazines

Wish book: Mail-order catalog.

Layin' off to: Planning to.

Swink: Lick; bit, as "She ain't done nary a swink of washin."

Life everlastin': Rabbit tobacco.

Makin's: Cigarette papers and smoking tobacco for roll-your-own smoking. The tobacco was in tin cans and muslin sacks with drawstrings and went by names including Bull Durham, RJR (Run John Run), and Golden Grain. Tobacco factories in Durham, North Carolina, were employing two hundred and fifty women in 1884 to make tobacco sacks. A sack-sewing machine was developed two years later, but the drawstrings still had to be inserted by hand; by 1906 women were getting paid thirty cents per thousand for the bags they strung.

Hoover dust: Smoking tobacco for roll-your-owns produced by the simple procedure of crushing cured leaves of scrap tobacco in one's hands. The name came from President Herbert Clark Hoover, then in office.

Dust an' paper: Makin's.

Prayer book: A book, or pack, of cigarette papers for building or rolling your own. Patrons of head shops call them papers, and rolling papers.

Gimmie paper: Same as above.

Tailormades; ready mades: Factory-made cigarettes.

Mountain joy: Snuff.

A little rub: A dip of snuff.

Bladder: A tube containing snuff.

Pig-twist auger: A twist of chewing tobacco. The imagery relates to the twist in a pig's tail and the turns in an auger.

Ambeer; ambia: Tobacco spittle. Sophisticated spitters never try to spit level against the wind.

Dusking: Hunting wild game at twilight.

Jacking; jack-lighting: Firelighting to attract and kill wild game. Wild game becomes easy prey at night when hunters blind them temporarily with lights. The practice began in these parts with Indians taking waterfowl. William Shakespeare called it "bat-fowling."

Lapping: Firelighting from a boat to take raccoons on banks of streams.

Virginia fence: Rail fence; worm fence; snake fence.

Bummers: General William Tecumseh Sherman's foragers and pillagers in a tour of Georgia. Henry W. Grady, Georgia editor and platform speaker, said of Sherman later: "Some people think he is a kind of careless man with fire."

Galvanized Yankee: One who in the Civil War was captured and took allegiance to the Confederacy and joined Confederate service.

Blue bellies: Yankees in general and Yankee troops in particular.

Blue backs: Confederate paper money.

Shucks: The lowest standard in monetary value; devalued paper currency of the Confederate states was worth no more than corn shucks or pea shucks.

Swamp dollar: An American copper cent, circa 1845. Similar in size and weight to the disenfranchised Susan B. Anthony dollar, the swamp dollar was customarily used in Southern rural areas to weight down the eyelids of recently deceased persons. Only a sorry person would steal pennies from a dead man's eyes.

Brozines, brozeens: Alabama and Mississippi plantation and sawmill tokens for trade only at plantation and sawmill stores and commissaries.

Doogaloo: Credit vouchers against upcoming pay in the Champion Fibre lumbering operations in old days in western North Carolina.

Beau dollars: Cartwheels; silver dollars.

Dobber: A float on a fishing line.
    Here is as good a place as any to tick off some of the most popular lures used for leisure fishing in Southern streams and ponds: Stick bait—cocoons undetached from twigs on which they were developed; Merita flies—damp bread rolled into small wads and wrapped around hooks; garden hackle—earthworms skewered on hooks.

Earwigs: Small centipedes.

Clutch: A setting—not a sitting—of eggs for hatching; a brood of young birds.

Got a notion to: When one considered doing something or other.

Got wind of: Discovered.

Only-est, onlest: The only one.

Church key: A one-piece can and bottle opener.

At that: A phrase to achieve sharper definition, or to intensify something already said, as, when charged with makin' out with another's husband, the accused lady bridled and sneered, "Him? Why, he's threatless as a mule—an' he's ugly, at that."

Norfolk War: The war of 1812.

Worked out, played out: Disappeared, as "The herrin' fishin' has jus' 'bout worked out in the Chowan river."

Listen at: Listen to.

Mirin' branch: A stream with a quicksand bottom.

All nine yards of it: The whole wad with all the trimmin's.

Took roundance: Circled, as one rounding a tree in a chase.

Keeley: Kelly pool, a pool hall game in which scoring is determined by a numbered pill taken from a box. Keeley pool got its name from the more familiar Keeley Institute, sectional resorts where well-fixed Southern topers matriculated to dry out in "the Keeley cure." Many patrons took the cure because of their "periodicals," their periodic drunken sprees.

Waitin' on: Waiting for, as in "I'm a-waitin' on you to make up yore cotton-pickin' mind."

Liked to: Almost; came near to, as in "He liked to turned Republican."

Give: Pay, as in "How much did you give for that bandbox heater."

Same old six and seven: The same as always—it still adds up to thirteen and no luck.

A-feared: Afraid.

Cotton to: Take a liking to; fancy.

Used to could; used to: Formerly.

Andy Jackson, hell an' thunder: An expression of elation, of feeling. The provenance and stomping ground of this expression is East Tennessee. When word of the American victory at New Orleans got back to Jonesboro, where Jackson had recently practiced law, the report said he had killed all the British troops and was on his way overseas to take possession of England.

"Whoopee! Hurrah for Andy Jackson! Hell an' thunder," an admirer shouted. "I knowed he could whup anybody that day I seed him ride that hoss-race at Greasy Cove."

That day at Greasy Cove was not one of Jackson's better ones. When he had come to Jonesboro from North Carolina he brought along a pretty fair race horse. Already on the scene was a mount belonging to Colonel Robert Love and winner over some of Virginia's fastest horses.

And now the almost inevitable race between the two was held at the Greasy Cove track near Erwin with hundreds of people, some bettors, attending. Jackson's jockey took sick just before the race was to begin, and Jackson rode in his stead. He lost, and he and Colonel Love exchanged harsh words and had a falling out. The Colonel called Jackson "a long, gangling, sorrel-topped soap stick," and Jackson made for him with his fists. Cooler heads prevailed and bloodshed was spared. But Jackson's reputation as a man with a short fuse was enhanced.

Let the buckets down: Quit searching, or wandering, and decide, as Brigham Young decided, that this is the place to stop and settle in for whatever project is called for.

Drive up a stob: Plant a figurative marker to signify or symbolize a promise or achievement, as in memorializing one who stood up and was counted in a significant political contest.

Eh law, aye law: Oh Lord, an interjection.

One of the greatest interjections ever devised to be noncommittal yet carry on a conversation is "eh law," and it is passing into oblivion. More's the pity.

"Eh law" doesn't say anything, but the speaker can interpret it as agreement and encouragement to go on. Yet the respondent with "eh law" is safe from misquotation.

My parents and their contemporaries used it, and I did, too, like this: "Did you see Sarah Finch getting into Tom Ball's buggy? What do you think of that?" "Eh law." "Sarah better watch her step." "Eh law." "I don't know what Sarah's folks are up to, letting her carry on so." "Eh law."

The expression was used to respond to opinions about political candidates, the price of tobacco, or crisis in Europe—Bill Sharpe in *The State Magazine*.

I can't dance and it's too wet to plow: Where do we go from here?

# This World and One More

*Breetherin', as bein' I'm here, I'll commence the meetin' fur Brother Buncombe, an' then he'll preach the funeral sarmint accordin' to previous app'intment. But while I'm here a-fore you, I want to say as how my main business over here is a-huntin' of some seed peas. An' if anybody here has got any to spar', I'd like to know it after meetin'."*

—*A preacher from afar engaged*
*in another mission*

Fine as snuff an' ain't half as dusty: Feelin' peart; bright an' sassy; as fine as frog hair; bright-eyed and bushy-tailed.

Peart: In good health and spirits and couldn't be better. Peart conveys the impression of numerous qualities—full of life, of a joyous and happy nature, sprightly, fresh, sassy, impudent, alert, intelligent.

200

Pearted up: If you weren't peart earlier, you improved with treatment. Maybe you got a sympathetic listener, or a bowl of hot pot likker with cornbread crumbled in it, or a dollop of peartenin' juice high in alcoholic content.

He can turn gravel: In robust health is one who, on urinating al fresco, produces a stream strong enough to tumble pebbles.

Fair to middlin': Able to crack corn; alive and well.

As good as common, as well as common: 'Bout like common; fair to middlin'.

Middlin' peart: In fair health.

Tol'able: Middlin'; moderate.

Kind of puny: Feeling less than common.

Kind of triflin': Same as above.

Middlin': Not in the best of health but not down sick either.

Ain't up to snuff: Puny like; po'ly; not well.

Drinlin': Puny; pindly; frail; in old age and decay; has seen best days.

Nerves, poor nerves, wore-out nerves: Mental trouble.

Nerve doctor: Psychiatrist.

Weary dismals: Doin' porely an' no two ways about it.

Puny aroun': To be ailing; indisposed; off one's feed.

Better than been a-bein': Has pearted up.

Enjoyin' poor health: The role of chronic complainers.

Down in the back: A misery in the back; with pain or stiffness in the back.

Tuckered out; plum' tuckered out: Wore out; petered out; exhausted; plum' tard.

Pegged out: Played out; fagged out; exhausted.

Cain't hardly go: About played out.

Cain't hardly git up an' down: Same as above.

Mighty shackly, shacklin': About to fall apart.

Fair whipped down: Same as above.

Rode hard an' put up wet: Same as above and with aches and pains; bone tard.

So tard you could scrape it off with a stick: Bone tard, as from barnin', or harvestin', tobacco all day.

Just up: Well.

So as to be about: Same as above.

Not very well: Ill.

Ain't much: Like nothin'; not feeling well.

Ain't nohow: No 'count; porely.

Droll: Unwell; lifeless.

Foolish: Frail.

Keeled up, laid up, got down: Incapacitated with sickness or injury.

Took hurt: Got injured.

Powerful weak: Weak as skimmed piss, as one after having hard chills and fever.

Phosphate gland: Prostate gland.

Low blood: Hypotension.

Aiguh: Ague; chills and fever.

Right smart shake: Malarial chills and fever.

Breakdown fever: Malarious fever; Dengue fever; influenza.

Country fever, swamp fever: Malaria.

Pneumonia fever: Pneumonia.

Bronze John, Yellow Jack: Yellow fever.

Asmy: Asthma.

Fetiddy: Asafetida.

Roaches of the liver: Cirrhosis.

Back set: Relapse.

Epizoodicks: Imaginary ailments.

Higulcian flips: An imaginary ailment indigenous to Texas.

All overs: Aggravated; where everything goes wrong; the mysterious ailment that felled Herbert Hyde's grandpa's cow.

All overish: Neither sick nor well but uncomfortable; a prelude to coming down with the flu.

Gok's disease: God only knows.

Down sick: Turned sick, as "He's down sick with the low blood."

Peak-ed: Sickly; emaciated in appearance and disposition.

Sulphur and molasses: A springtime medicine to cure one of a peak-ed condition.

Workin' medicine: Epsom salts.

Wormin' out medicine: Chewing tobacco.

Freegies vermifuge: A springtime medicine, usually for children suspected of being infested with tapeworms and hookworms. Made from oil of Jerusalem oak seed.

Cotton seed tea: A household remedy favored by Andrew Jackson for treatment of whooping cough.

Mergens of medications: Enough medicines to cure a colicky colt.

Misput: Out of sorts; aggravated; pouty; put out.

Complains of feeling better: She'd been punyin' aroun' earlier an' was barely able to take vittles.

Draggly: Bedraggled; drag-assed; drearisome.

Shabby: When you feel you've been sent for and cain't go.

Pizzlesprung: Pooped.

Against: Injurious, as in "Eatin' rootybaggers is against me."

Outish: In need of a drink to take the wind off the stomach.

Feelin' wormy: Sickly.

Fall off: Lose weight.

Gant: Gaunt.

Like a gutted herring: Gaunt and run down.

Graveyard cough: A hacking cough.

Green apple two-step: Backdoor trots; tourist sickness.

Bloody flux: Dysentery.

Runnin' off: Diarrhea.

Backed up: Constipated.

Liverish: Yeller janders; jaundice.

So sick he threw up his socks: His stomach was wamblin' or he felt nauseous.

Fell to the bed, tuck to the bed, took down sick: Became ill and went to bed.

Layin' up: Malingering; loafing.

Under the doctor: In the care of a physician. One who "waits on sickness" is a nurse.

Fidges: A nervous feeling.

Budgies: Annoying abberrations or disorders associated with the nervous and circulatory systems, with involuntary jerking in one's legs and occasional slight and transient pains that you can't put your hands on.

Climbing fits: Tremors while sleeping.

Stew around: Engage in nervous activity.

Nigh in a franzy: Worried and almost frantic.

Weak trembles: Weak and wobbly because of hunger or apprehension.

Mollygrubs, mulligrubs: Slightly unwell; upset; having the blues; cross; cranky.

Gone to pieces: All tore up; distressed.

Uneases: Disturbs, as in "Light'nin' an' thunder uneases my dog."

Smarts: Soreness; slight pain.

Fitified: Epileptic; subject to convulsions.

Hitch in the git-along: An impediment in gait.

Twinges: Arthritis. Cures for twinges in the hinges include toting a buckeye, and taking a tonic of pokeberry juice and corn whiskey—the juice of one pokeberry to a gallon of whiskey.

Give out: To lose hope, to fail; become exhausted; worn out; fagged out; played out, as in "I'm plum' give out from a-grubbin' that air new ground."

Fair whipped down: Debilitated almost as much as above.

Swaged down, shrunk up: Reduced in size, as with a boil.

Spoiled by sunshine: Had a sunstroke.

Monkeys: What field hands get when heat gets the best of them.

Havin' a dog fit: A conniption fit; upset and agitated.

Hard fit: A tantrum.

All broke up, all tore up: Distressed; also, laughing like crazy.

In a strut, in a swivet, in a sweat: Under strain; hard pressed.

In a tight, in a fix, in a mess: Having a problem; in a dilemma; caught between a rock and a hard place; caught where the wool is short.

In the go long: Upset; frustrated; when you can't get a-holt of yourself.

Mattered up: Eyelids glued shut of a morning.

Road rash: Motorcyclists' term for red ass.

Don't worry it: Don't pick at a scab or a sore.

Punishing: Hurting, as "My eyetooth's punishin' me somethin' turbl."

Bealing: A boil.

Bealed head: A swollen face.

Pump knot: A swelling on the head, often from a clout.

Took a turn: Changed condition for better or worse.

In low cotton: In depression; morbid; in the dismals; low in spirit.

Down in the dumps: Sad; dispirited; melancholy; with heaviness of heart.

Disencouraging: Pessimistic; out of heart; down in the mouth.

Dolesome: Sad; worried.

Dauncy, daunsy: Moody; depressed.

Take on: Grieve; become hysterical.

Keep your dobbers up: Keep up your courage; don't be out of heart; keep your pecker up. "Faint heart," said Lindsey Nelson, "ne'er screwed the cook."

Wearies: Worries; bad nerves.

Bad off: In bad shape, mentally, physically, financially; hardly keeping body and soul together.

Heart sick: Very sick; so sick he's quit cussin'.

Ageable: No spring chicken.

Gittin' on: Aging.

Might last through one more clean shirt: Getting on in years; failing.

Dotey: Senile.

On the go down, slowed back: In declining health; ain't gonna hold out or survive.

Dwindles: A wasting away, as in "He's dying of the dwindles."

About to poot the rug: In the last threshing; in the last of pea time.

Pickin' at the bed covers: Floccillation; same as above.

Standin' on the drop edge of yonder: About to peg out; about to hang it up.

Right at the hinge creak of death: At the very rim edge.

Long in the neck: Ain't long for this world.

His body is stiffenin', his breath is slackin' in his throat: He's on his last.

He's gittin cold from the feet up, his eyes are set, he's in a death chill: Same as above.

Goin' through the gate, has seen the river: Dying.

Jumped the buckeye log, set his bucket down, faded: Died; the spirit had fled.

Rung the knell, finished out the row: Said "good mornin'" to Saint Peter.

Died all at once: Died a sudden death.

Laid out: The corpse is prepared for burial, usually having been bathed and dressed, or shrouded, by neighbors.

Lay corpse: A body laid out and awaiting burial.

Settin' up with: Keeping the corpse company during the night at the stay place of the deceased.

Graveyard ground: Cemetery; place of burial.

Put under: Bury.

Funeralize: Eulogize in a preachin' funeral.

Preachin' funeral: If bad weather or other adverse conditions prevailed when the burial was held, the preachin' funeral came later. Often in autumn when crops had been laid by, creeks were low, and relatives and friends had ample and proper time for last rites.

Years often passed between burying and funeraliz-ing. Once, in Kentucky, a preachin' funeral was held for a man and, simultaneously, for his four deceased wives.

Treed and mowed: What a well tended graveyard ground should be.

## And the Very Last Page and Entry

That's the last button off Gabe's britches: That's the last shingle on the barn; slap out of; that's the end of the ballgame; that's all she wrote; it's too wet to plow; we've wound up our ball of yarn; that's all, y'all.

And that's about the size of it.

# Thanky Note

Many friends are due thanks for help in construction of this collation of colloquialisms, regionalisms, folk speech—this categorized, unexpurgated, illustrated assortment of Southern fried words and phrases.

Especially appreciated are contributions from members of the Cotton States Literary Board. Unregistered and undocumented, ephemeral and mercurial, the Cotton States Literary Board is a shackly confederacy of students of the hand-me-down, patched-up, deep-fried, warmed-over, and made-on-the-spot speech of the South—speech that is nourished by corn bread and tempered by corn whiskey.

We thank in particular a trio of card-carrying scholars with expertise in folkways and folksay—Dr. Cratis Williams, W. Amos (Doc) Abrams, and John Parris. In the fields of folklore and folk speech, they stand tall. Oftentimes in development of this word-working project they were first in line with contributions and, conversely, were the last resort in matters of definition, derivation, legitimacy, authenticity. Less scholarly, perhaps, but not a smidgen less valuable were Charles Silas Edwards and Russell T. Clay. Many words and phrases that otherwise may have been lost to the printed page and the collected lore of the land now come to you through their courtesy and interest.

For helping us develop better appreciation for the fine-tuning of words and phrases—by blue-penciling, by setting examples, by word-of-mouth exchanges in companionable pursuits—we raise a glass once again to good and articulate companions in diverse endeavors: to John Lardner, Walt Kelly, Joseph Mitchell, O. J. Coffin, James R. McIver, Lessing L. Engelking, Robert W. Madry, Edwin M. Lanham, A. J. Leibling, Phillips Russell, John Crosby, W. C. Heinz, Don Whitehead, Walter Wellesley (Red) Smith, Edward Tatum Wallace, H. Allen Smith, Larry Smits, Robert Ruark, Curtis G. (Bill) Pepper, Art Smith, Robert B. Peck, Gerald Howard, Edwin S. McIntosh, Robert Mason, Clifton Daniel, Marion Cyrenus Blackman.

We thank Lindsey Nelson, Hal Boyle, Frank L. Wilder, Kenneth Koyen, Paul K. Lee, Leo Corcoran, Kenneth W. Bilby, E. Sanford Verry, Dan T. Winter IV, Dick Bothwell, Ivie Wilder, Kenneth H. Winter, Harold Fredericks, Mary Crosby, Sam Ragan, Peggy Mann, Charles Verrill, C. K. S. Dodd, Bobs Pinkerton, Charles F. Vance, Jr., Lee Wilder, Cliff Sandersen, W. E. Horner, Marshall E. Newton, Malcolm E. Bell, Jr., W. Kerr Scott, Carl Levin, Terry Sanford, Robert J. Donovan, Burke Davis, Russell A. Swindell, Frank Porter Graham, Sam Brightman, Larry LeSueur, Ivy Fischer Stone, Fifi Oscard, Nat Benchley, Jack Aulis, Aage Woldike.

Also, J. Gordon Fraser, Palmer Maples, David P. Murray, Mary Cole, Michael Montgomery, Nancy McDonough, Herbert M. McCallum, Marjorie Barnitz, George F. Scheer, Sam Dominick, Nell Joslin Styron, William W. Speight, W. G. Wells, Robert W. Scott, Sue Henry, John M. Redding, Allen C. Barbee, Don Wharton, Jean and Gus Harer, Bill Vaughan, Nancy Clatworthy,

William McWhorter Cochrane, J. R. (Cotton) Hildreth, Holmes
G. Paulin, Ben E. Roney, Woodrow Price, Wilton Kelly, Peggy
W. Satterfield, Edgar Sparks, Clary Thompson, Ned Huffman.

Also, Robert Burton House, Weldon B. Denny, Guy Munger,
Thomas J. Nixon III, Dan Lohwasser, Casey Dempsey, H. G.
Jones, Oscar F. Smith, E. H. (Duck) Lewis, Wright Bryan, Eliz-
abeth Kytle, Jack Leland, Helen Brodie, Bud Alexander, Bill
Ballard, Manly Wade Wellman, William S. Powell, Kemper H.
Hyers, Larry Pollard, Odell C. Kimbrell, Opie L. Shelton,
Rogers Whitener, J. D. Wilson, Jay Jenkins, Jack E. Daugherty,
Norvell E. Oden, Susan K. Gordon, David Moffett, Dorothy
Briley, John Teany, Richard Kluger, James Morton Smith, A. C.
Greene, William A. Drake, W. K. McNeil, Nat C. Hughes, Joe
Creason, Cyrus B. King, David B. Gracy II, Cynthia J. Beeman,
Gerald George, Nell LoPresti, John B. Funderburg, Terry W.
Lipscomb, John Ehle.

Also, John E. Steely, Braxton Flye, Simmons Fentress, War-
ren W. Hassler, Jr., Kermit Hunter, William J. Brinn, Richard F.
Knapp, John S. Heiser, Carl Carson, Charles Aycock Poe,
Thomas McGowan, Carolyn B. Farr, William M. Ewald, Fern K.
Myllenbeck, J. Edgar Kirk, Lou Clemmons, Carlton Combs, Jr.,
Thomas W. Lambeth, Al Rodriguez, Joan Burkart, Hoke Norris,
Jerry C. Cashion, William C. Friday, Letty Wilder, Charles E.
Lee, B. W. C. Roberts, George Core, Lucille Truitt, Dortha C.
Frank, Ruth Barbour, James M. Poyner.

Also, Zora Neale Hurston, Joseph R. Bateman, Jr., Norman
E. Eliason, W. Inman Reed, William Murchison, Charles Clay,
William S. Price, Jr., Bud Wachtel, Chris Morton, Horton Mills,
Richard J. Gonder, Lois Smathers Neale, Ernie Williamson,
Hugh Morton, Robert W. Auman, Arlene M. Haywood, Roland
Giduz, Myrlene W. Tye, Billy Arthur, Eula Mae Edwards, Martha
E. Battle, A. C. Snow, Helen Fernald, Panky Snow, James Ross,
Basil Sherrill, Carl Quattlebaum, Joe B. Frantz, G. Andrew
Jones, Mabel C. Simmons, William B. Wright, Inglis Fletcher,
Dan K. Moore, Ruth H. Roberson, Judith A. Schiff, Hugh Buck-

ner Johnston, Eugenia Rawls, Bill NcNutt, Charles C. Funder-
burk, Frank R. Gilchrist, George P. Wilson, Ramon F. Adams,
Lee Smith, H. J. Dudley, Roger Brantley, Jurgen Abel, Freeman
Chum, Edmund L. Engel, Laura Messer Scott, J. Bryan III,
China Blanche Cordell Hicks Sebastian, A. K. A. China Cordell
Hicks.

# Publick Notice

Readers of *You All Spoken Here* are cordially invited to put down on paper and pass along to the publisher, Viking Penguin Inc., 40 West 23d Street, New York, New York 10010, additional items of Southern speech that may be considered for inclusion in a revised edition, down the path, of this job of word work. The language of the South is a viable language, as you may have discovered, with new words and phrases constantly being contrived and added to the plunder room of Southern talk. Those are what we want. We also want the old—the pertinent words and phrases that somehow got overlooked or escaped attention altogether in the compiling of this collection—regionalisms, colloquialisms, family talk.

We want to have a look and a listen at additional material, and hope you will oblige.

It will be a pleasure to do business with you.